£2.50

CHAUCER'S
BOOK OF FAME

The Triumph of Fame

From a tapestry now in the Kunsthistorisches Museum, Vienna (see p. 129, n. 1).

CHAUCER'S
BOOK OF FAME

AN EXPOSITION OF
'THE HOUSE OF FAME'

J. A. W. BENNETT

OXFORD
AT THE CLARENDON PRESS
1968

Oxford University Press, Ely House, London W. 1

GLASGOW NEW YORK TORONTO MELBOURNE WELLINGTON
CAPE TOWN SALISBURY IBADAN NAIROBI LUSAKA ADDIS ABABA
BOMBAY CALCUTTA MADRAS KARACHI LAHORE DACCA
KUALA LUMPUR HONG KONG TOKYO

PRINTED IN GREAT BRITAIN

Preface

SINCE this book went to press a study of *Chaucer and the Tradition of Fame* by B. G. Koonce has appeared under the Princeton imprint. It therefore behoves me to state that the following chapters contain the substance of a course of lectures delivered in Oxford in 1960. Although Mr. Koonce's views on certain passages coincide with mine, an ocean of differences divides our main assumptions and conclusions. I reserve my comments on his interpretation for a forthcoming edition of the poem, which will also include full bibliographical references and detailed discussion of points and problems here treated cursorily or not at all.

For enlightenment on the iconography of Venus and on 'ecphrasis' as a literary device I owe much to my friends and former pupils, Margaret Twycross and John Norton-Smith. But I have refrained from drawing on the discussions of these topics in their Oxford dissertations.

J. A. W. BENNETT

Magdalene College
Cambridge

Contents

Introduction

The Book of Fame—to accept Chaucer's final title, and Caxton's, rather than the more usual form, which is sanctioned largely by its use in *The Legend of Good Women*— was admired by poets as different as Spenser and Pope; Warton saw in it 'great strokes of Gothick imagination'— a phrase worth pondering. But more recent critics have been loath to regard it as more than a diversion, a *divertisse-ment*. They consider it a ramshackle structure, as full of 'gigges' and 'chirkinges' as the house of twigs described in it; giddymaking, discursive, miscellaneous. Some will admit its lively incidentals—in one of which they profess to get a glimpse of the poet's life as a henpecked husband— or its sallies of the humour that is accounted typically Chaucerian. But most commentators seem to be of some-what the same mind as the seventeenth-century owner of the Fairfax MS. of the poem, who scribbled on the flyleaf that he bought it 'intending to exchange it for a better book'. W. P. Ker went so far as to claim that the poem was not 'honest' and not a specimen of Chaucer's art.

Such a forthright criticism as Ker's may prove more salutary by its very provocativeness than the concessive kind that will grant the zest and piquancy of certain parts but will dismiss the rest as a failure, lacking shape or sym-metry, and will quote Chaucer's own supposed disclaimer that he was here intent on 'art poetical'. A study of the context in which that phrase occurs will show that he is there at once making game of his readers, and obeying the rules of a very sophisticated medieval poetic. Once we recognize this sophistication as pervading the whole poem we shall read it with fresh eyes. Never was Chaucer more sure of himself than when he professed at the beginning of its third book 'that I do no diligence To shewe craft'. 'Craft' and 'curiositee', significantly recurrent terms, are in more than one sense at the very heart of the work. And never was his art more deliberate than when he constructed this supremely architectural poem, in which each theme is treated in architectonic and constructional terms. He was so sure of himself that he dared to play irreverent variations on motifs drawn from his supreme masters in poetry and morality—Dante and Boethius—yet without modifying his or our view of either; so sure of himself that he could afford to begin with a long-drawn-out *dubitatio* which leaves *him* breathless and makes casual modern readers wonder what they are in for. Even while we hurry after those quick octosyllabics we are being attuned to the dominant *allegro* of the poem proper. Speed—sometimes bewildering speed —crowded scenes, swift action, and swift change—these belong equally to each part of the poem as they belong to the lofty lady who sits at the centre of it.

The late appearance of this 'goddesse of renown and of fame' is a cause of uneasiness to those critics who attach too much importance to the traditional title, and Pope, planning his imitative *Temple of Fame*, could find no use for the first thousand lines of his exemplar. But attentive reading will alter this judgement and reveal that fame, in its many-sided medieval sense (which is not altogether the same as the Augustan) is unmistakably present as a motif in the first main movement, the Virgilian. It is linked there with the theme of 'tidings' of lovers—'these ilke lovers' whose presence in the Proem on dreams (37) might other-wise seem casual or unpremeditated; and it is in fulfilment of a promise of further such tidings that the dreamer is later carried to Fame's palace. The initial surface-sense of confusion is no more than a preparative for such complex filiations. Nowhere should we be content with a literal reading. The very book in which the poet proposes to eschew the poetic art is in part devoted to enumerating the great poets of old time, and essentially to the discovery of new poetic *matière*. In one sense the whole work is a vindication of poetry. But those ancient poets securely perched on their pillars in Fame's temple are not introduced arbitrarily: with one exception they are the same poets on whom the whole Trojan-Roman sequence of the opening book is based—Virgil, Ovid, Claudian, Lucan. Venus may seem to have naught to do with Fame. But it is in her temple that we first hear the word and that we are shown a Dido who falls a victim to both Fame and Love. The temple of Venus and the house of Fame are consciously juxtaposed.

The appearance at the outset of the poem of a naked Venus might seem to be a Renaissance anticipation and might prompt comparison with Botticelli's Venere rising from the waves. For the Renaissance is now immutably associated with the restoration and rediscovery of classical statuary and a pagan aesthetic; whilst the attention Chaucer gives elsewhere to this nude goddess as depicted by Boccaccio might appear to confirm the impression that his sympathies would lie with the Italians of the new era. But in fact Chaucer's Venus, like his Virgil, belongs firmly to the Middle Ages. It is one purpose of the present study to show that his iconographic learning, like his scientific lore, was traditional rather than novel and far removed from the Florentine platonism that was Botticelli's inspiration. It is in presenting the monstrous yet

majestical figure of Fame hymned by all the Muses that
Chaucer most nearly approached the Renaissance—and
indeed rivalled Petrarch. His presentation of Fame is more
lively and more colourful than that in the *Trionfi*; and
Petrarch's catalogue of the Famous—a miscellany of
Roman heroes and Greek philosophers—is tedious by
comparison with Chaucer's select list. Petrarch's work,
moreover, like the closing pages of Boccaccio's *De
Genealogia Deorum*, betrays a personal preoccupation with
fame which is closer to the feeling of Horace's *Exegi
monumentum aere perennius* than to the English writer's
modest and unselfconscious invocation of Apollo. We
shall see that Chaucer may well owe one of his images of
Fame to the *Trionfi*; but in the role he assigns to poets
as sole preservers of men's fame he anticipates Ariosto. If
the theme of fame later attracted the greatest English poets
it was in part because of the compelling figure of Chaucer's
'noble quene'. In *Lycidas* the Phoebus whom Chaucer
invoked, and not in vain, merely gives a firmer enunciation
of the doctrine implicit in his poem:

> Fame is no plant that grows on mortal soil
> Nor in the glistering foil
> Set off to the world, nor in Broad Rumour lies,
> But lives and spreds aloft by those pure eyes
> And perfet witness of alljudging Jove

—the same Jove to whose 'grace' Chaucer too had owed
his glimpse of Fame's real nature. Critics have teased
themselves over the identity of the 'man of gret auctorite'
who appears just as Chaucer's poem breaks off. The
dreamer himself, we ought to remember, could not
identify him. But 'auctorite' indicates that he is an *auctor*,
perhaps one of the 'grete clerkes' invoked at the outset of so

many of Chaucer's poems, including this one, and prominent in the temple of Fame itself. His mere presence may imply that the Boethian sentiments which colour the centre of the work are not to be ignored; and if spelt out their terms would resemble Milton's: 'Leave final judge-ments to Jove; turn your mind to the rich harvest of story that is yet to reap; in the practice of poetry itself there is more lasting solace than in devotion to Cupid or to the bitch goddess of Fame.' Yet before reading all this into 'auctorite' we must also remember that elsewhere Chaucer gives the word deeply ironical colour: in *Troilus* it is the calculating Calcas who is 'a lord of gret auctorite' and 'a gret devyn, in science so expert' (*Tr.* i. 65–67).

It is tantalizing that the swift movement of the poem stops abruptly, before the poet's dream is over. But we must beware of reading back into the early part of the work our disappointment at this lack of formal conclusion. That we have practically reached the end of the *action* is plainly suggested. And if we have read other dream-poems, and Chaucer's in particular, we know what the formal end would have been like. Usually the dreaming poet is awakened by an external sound that corresponds to some noise or alarum in the dream itself; thus the shouting of the birds in the *Parliament* echoes a dawn chorus, and the castle-bell in the *Book of the Duchess* sounds within the dream the hours struck by the bell that wakes the sleeping poet. Conceivably the poet stopped at this point just because a conventional conclusion of that kind would have made for sameness. In the nature of the case, more-over, such a conclusion is likely to be quiet and relaxed, even, one might say, tame: 'This was my sweven; now it is doon'; 'I wok and othere bokes tok me to To rede upon . . .'; whereas the whole point of the final scene in *Fame*

is that the whirligig of Rumour never ceases its swift
gyrations: the tidings increase 'evermo As fir is wont to
quikke and go' (2078, cf. 2118). Winged words fly about
in their thousands; tale-tellers climb and clamber pell-
mell. And the dreamer outpaces them all. If it is right to
interpret this haste as suggestive and symbolic of the
urgency of the poet who in the 'entremedling' of pilgrims'
tidings sees the very vista of the Canterbury Tales themselves spreading out before him; if he has indeed glimpsed
the 'foyson' of stories, the plenty of 'alle the sheves in the
lathe'—then we can well forgo the satisfaction of a fully
rounded dream. And if an exegesis of the work as it stands
compels us to reshape our notions of the limits of 'gothick'
learning and imagination, then, whatever our final judgement as to the poet's success in divining the nature and
attributes of Fame, this study will have been amply justified.

CHAPTER I

Venus and Virgil

He was evir (God wait) all womanis frend
GAVIN DOUGLAS on 'my mastir Chaucer'

I

'GOD turne us every dreme to goode! . . .' The tone,
casual, conversational, intimate, of these opening lines;
the light metre; the ostensible concern with the significance
of dreams; the immediate introduction of the bemused
poet in the first person: all these features call to mind the
like opening of the *Book of the Duchess*, which stands next
to the *Fame* in that recital of works claimed by Alceste,
in the Prologue to the *Legend of Good Women* (F. 415–23),
to have been written in praise of Cupid. In the prefaces
to all three poems the style and attitude are unpretentious:
at once we are on equal terms with the narrator, who
buttonholes us with a 'I wol yow tel' or a 'wel ye wot',
inducing us to share his bafflement and his ignorance. His
confession 'Myselven can not telle why' (*Book of the Duchess*,
34) is here echoed by such phrases as 'I noot... ne can hem
noght... why the cause is, noght wot I'. It will thus be no
surprise to find him later described as a 'lewed man' (866);
and he soon deliberately distances himself from the 'grete
clerkes' (53). The repeated suggestion that the causes of
dreams are mysterious (12 ff.) prepares us for entry into a
world of wonders, both natural and fantastic, just as in the
Parliament of Fowls the 'miracles' of Cupid (*PF*, 11) form

prelude to a dream of love and lovers. Here dreams themselves are described as 'miracles' (12); a reminder that in
medieval poetry the miraculous world of love is almost
conterminous with the world of dream. For Chaucer they
are both worlds of paradox.

Of the identity of these two worlds proof lies to hand in
the supreme textbook of love *paramour*, the *Roman de la
Rose*. It is through the gate of dream that the lover in that
poem comes to the wonderful garden; but before describing
it he ponders, just as Chaucer is here doing, on the
veracity of dreams in general:

> Maintes genz dient qu'en songes
> N'a se fables non e mençonges . . .

Even though Chaucer is more reserved than Guillaume
de Lorris—who goes on to cite Macrobius's view that not
all dreams are 'false ne lees'—he has certainly patterned his
opening on that of the *Roman* which he had himself translated; and he knew likewise Jean de Meun's continuation
of the poem, in which Nature discourses (*multa inter alia*)
on lovers' wishful or fearful dreams, in terms that Chaucer
borrows both here and in the *Parliament*. Yet even Nature
will not commit herself:

> Ne ne revueil dire des songes
> S'il sont veir ou s'il sont mençonges;
> Se l'en les deit dou tout eslire,
> Ou s'il font dou tout a despire;
> Pourquei li un sont plus orrible,
> Plus bel li autre e plus paisible,
> Selonc leur aparicions
> En diverses complexions,
> E selonc les divers courages
> Des meurs divers e des aages;

Ou se Deus par teus visions
Enveie revelacions,
Ou li malignes esperiz,
Pour metre les genz es periz . . .
(RR, 18499–512)[1]

But it is not solely love poetry that takes dream for its province. Dante's *Commedia* and Langland's *Piers Plow-man* show not merely that the profoundest spiritual state-ments could be expressed in terms of dream, but also that verse was thought to be the proper mode in which to make such statements. Thus dream and poetry are as closely 'intermeddled' as the winged tidings that are to appear at the very end of *Fame* (2118). And Chaucer will very shortly invoke the god of sleep (and of dream: 80) with a devoutness not unlike that found in his later pleas to Venus and the Muses (518–22) and to the god of poetry himself (1091 ff.). The long initial consideration of the sources and nature of dreams ceases to seem irrelevant or inordinate when regarded as a prelude to the one work of the poet that dwells on the nature and rewards of poetic achievement; the work in which he follows in the foot-steps of poetry's two greatest princes (Virgil and Dante) and gives due honour and regard to lesser writers; the work in which he presents himself as a seeker after fresh poetic inspiration, new poetic 'tidings'. Such a quest, Professor Northrop Frye might argue, is properly cast in a dream form since dream often embodies 'the search of the libido or desiring self for a fulfilment that will deliver it from the anxieties of reality, but will still contain that reality'.[2]

---

[1] Chaucer draws on an adjacent passage from the *Roman* in *Fame*, 916 ff.: see below, p. 88.

[2] Northrop Frye, *Anatomy of Criticism* (Princeton, 1957), p. 193.

To stop to analyse the doctrine of these sixty lines of breathless introduction would be to obscure in a cloud of dream-psychology their ulterior significance, and to dull the effect of this firework display of various suggestion, terse allusion, and ambiguous syntax, in establishing the quick and sometimes jerky tempo that is to characterize the poem as a whole. Trajectories of vivid phrases will interlace throughout the work and intensify the effect of continual movement. So fast is the pace that we almost miss the seemingly casual glance at 'the cruel lyf unsofte Whiche these ilke lovers leden' (36–37); it will seem less casual when we notice that in the prime source of all medieval dream-lore, Macrobius's Commentary on Cicero's *Somnium Scipionis*, the account of *insomnia* hangs directly on two verses in Virgil, one of which comes from the same narrative of painful love that Chaucer is to picture in his dream of Venus's temple:

> Anna soror, quae me suspensam insomnia terrent!
>
> (*Aen*. iv. 9)

And though the speech of Dido beginning with this line cannot (for a very good reason) figure in that dream, it does appear in the *Legend of Good Women*: 'Now, dere sister myn, what may it be That me agasteth in my dreme? . . .' (F. 1170–81).[1] The allusion to love's cruelty in the Pro-logue is indeed premonitory of the first incidents of the dream, soon to be narrated, concerning the Dido story; and fifty lines later it is reinforced by the prayer that lovers may be shielded from 'unhappe and eche disese' (89)—from such mishap, in short, as we are to see befalling Dido.

---

[1] Cf. Macrobius, *Comm. In Somn. Scip*. I. iii. 6. *LGW*, F. 103–6 ('My besy gost . . . constreyned me . . . That in myn herte I feele yet the fir') was evidently suggested by Dido's *solus hic inflexit sensus . . . agnosco veteris vestigia flammae* (*Aen*. iv. 22–23).

Moreover, when at the end of the *Aeneid*-sequence the dreamer prays also to be saved 'fro fantom and illusioun' (493), the explanation of *insomnia* in Macrobius will prove pertinent to the 'illusions' in question. The motif will reappear in the second movement of the poem when the eagle, observing that Chaucer lacks tidings 'Of Loves folk, if they be *glade*' (645), promises amongst other 'wonder thinges' a glimpse of such lovers

> Whyl that they finde love of stele,
> *As thinketh hem . . .*
> And eke mo holdinge in hondes [in suspense]
>
> .   .   .   .   .   .
>
> And eke of loves mo eschaunges . . .   (674 ff.)

Meanwhile the jaunty near-pyrrhonism of the proem is hinting that, however traditional its terminology and patterning may be, we should be prepared for develop-ments that may be far from conventional. And there is a suggestion of parody in the concluding avowal that no one has ever dreamt

> So wonderful a dreme as I
> The tenthe day now of Decembre;   (62–63)

a playful variant of an ancient *topos* that Chaucer had learnt from Horace and found in Boccaccio. The specifying of a date is perhaps not, strictly speaking, part of the parody. Though dreams of love or wonder are customarily set in the spring or summer, at least one extant vision poem—Froissart's *Le Joli Buisson de Jonece*—names the year's mid-night as the time of a dream (30 November 1373). There is a touch here of the purposed ambiguity that pervades a similar allusion, in *The Parliament of Fowls*, to the time when he began his 'sweven for to write'.[1]

[1] *PF*, 117–19.

Something of the mock-serious subsists in the preliminary invocation to Morpheus next following. With
'*special* devocioun' he prays to this god 'that I of *rede*' (77);
and the interposed description (out of Ovid) of the god's
dwelling adds to the bookishness of the prayer. Chaucer
could have found classical precedent for such an arch
address to a deity in Horace (*Sat.* 1. 5. 53) or Ovid (*Ars
Amatoria*, ii. 704), but the quizzical reservation implied in
'*if* every dreme stonde in his might' (80) is his own device
—and one the point of which escaped the author of the Lyd-
gatian *Assembly of Gods*, who describes Morpheus, 'shewer
of dremes', as dwelling in the corner called Fantasy (l. 35).
The account of Sleep's cave of stone patently follows Ovid
(*Metamorphoses*, xi. 592–604), yet it hardly overlaps with the
memorable rendering in the *Book of the Duchess* of the story
of Alcione to which those lines in Ovid belong.[1] The few
un-Ovidian details are faintly flippant in their understate-
ment: thus the flood of hell is 'unswete', the god 'unmerie'.
This is hardly the care-charming Morpheus praised by
Froissart in his thirty-third Ballade nor 'le doulc dieu de
dormir' of whom he speaks in *L'Espinette Amoureuse* (3019).
For Froissart Morpheus is primarily the god who provides
love-visions:

[1] *BD*, 155–77—a set-piece in near-Renaissance style that caught Spenser's
eye: see *Faerie Queene*, I. i. 39–41.
Three of Ovid's similes that Chaucer had no occasion to use in his accounts
of Morpheus he inserts at different points in *Fame*:
>   Somnia varia iacent totidem, quot messis aristas,
>   silva gerit frondes, eiectas litus harenas. (*Met.* xi. 614–15)
Cf. *Fame*, 692, 'mo . . . then greynes be of sondes'; 1946, 'as fele as leves been on
trees'; 698, 'mo . . . then ever cornes were in graunges'.
Statius amplifies Ovid's description of Morpheus's home and specifies, like
Chaucer (*HF*, 70) that it is 'of stoon' (*cavis grave rupibus antrum*: *Theb.* x. 86);
within are carved shapes: *vaga somnia vultu, Vera simul fallsis permixtaque tristia
blandis*.

Morpheus le dieu dormant
Par lequel tout li vrai amant
Sont conforté, et c'est raisons,
En songes et en visions.
(*Le Paradys D'Amour*, 1718–21)

Chaucer soon alludes to just such solace (83–86); attribut⁄
ing it, however, not to Morpheus but to the Christian
deity as characterized by Dante in the opening phrase of
the *Paradiso*: 'colui che tutto move'—here rendered as
'he that movere is of al' (81). And with this glance at the
Commedia, the first of many, comes a slight change in tone
and tempo. To be paradoxical here would be profane; and
the wish that God may bless his hearers and in particular
the lovers among them is hardly less serious than his plea
at the beginning of *Troilus* that his readers should pray
'God . . . sende hem [viz. lovers] myght hire ladies so to
plese That it to love be worship and plesaunce' (*Tr.* i. 45–46:
an alteration of *Il Filostrato*). The insertion of a line from
Dante will the less surprise us if we recall the context of his
phrase—an invocation before he tells of his heavenly jour⁄
ney. In dream Chaucer is to make a similar ascent (and
when in describing it will turn at least twice to this very
canto). Yet the succeeding malediction on whosoever
misjudges his 'sweven' ('Dreme he barefot, dreme he
shod') tips the scales back to pleasantry. We are in fact
being juggled between high style and low, jest and earnest.
It is like an exercise in prosopopeia, in the Spanish sense
of 'Afectación de gravedad y pompa'. Yet it is more than
a *jeu d'esprit*. The pseudo⁄sinister reference (105) to the
avisioun of Croesus, the pre⁄eminent 'misdeemer' of dreams,
who dismissed Phanias's reading of his *somnium* as a 'fausse
glose'[1]—this reference deftly ties the invocation to the

---

[1] *RR*, 6489–620; cf. *CT*, B². 3917 ff.

opening questions about *avisiouns* and *revelaciouns*, and at the same time signals that our interest is to be extended from classical mythology to classical story.

II

Dreamers in literature have the privilege of falling asleep on the slightest provocation. The poet of *Piers Plowman*, waking in mid-morning after one dream, is seized by drowsiness 'er I hadde faren a fourlonge', and forthwith sleeps, to dream again (Passus V. B. 5 ff.). That Chaucer had in mind literary dreams as he describes the occasion of his 'sweven' is suggested by 'as I was wont to done' (113), the very words he had used to render the 'si con je soloie' in similar context at the opening of the *Roman* (cf. *Romaunt* 24). His likening of himself to a pilgrim worn out by a mere two-mile walk, his punning allusion (118) to the variant form of St. Leonard's name (Lithe-nard) are the last flickers of preliminary fun. The emphatic adversative 'But' (119) announces a change and takes us at one bound into the temple of his dream, which (and this implies some knowledge of iconography on his part) he at once recognizes as Venus's. Like most visionary places it is unlocalizable (129), yet far from being im-material—indeed it has many more golden images, rich tabernacles, pinnacles, figures 'than I had ever seen' (127). For Chaucer the world of dream—just because it is for him the world of poetry—always represents a heightening and intensifying of ordinary experience. In the *Parliament* the wood he dreams of is full of all manner of trees (172 ff.), air, earth, and sea are crowded with all manner of birds; in the *Book of the Duchess* the forest beasts are so abundant that no man could number them

(434–42); and thronged scenes and settings will recur throughout this poem, till we come at the end to another kind of building, crammed with travellers, each with scrip full to bursting.

A sense of richness rather than a clear visual impression is (with one important exception) what Chaucer's summary account of the interior of the temple conveys. For much more elaborate and formal descriptions of ornate buildings he could have found ample precedent, and he himself was to contribute to this literary tradition of 'ecphrasis' later in this very poem, as well as in his Knight's account of Theseus's theatre, with its gates of 'marbul white' and its oratories for Diana ('of alabastre white and reed coral'), Mars, and Venus, each with its 'noble kerving', 'portreitures', and figures (*CT*, A. 1885–1917, etc.). We owe such set pieces ultimately to Ovid's description of the palace of the sun with its gleaming columns of bronze and gold, its gables of ivory, its silver historiated doors (*Metamorphoses*, ii. 1–18: part of the tale of Phaeton to which Chaucer will allude later in *Fame*). But more pertinent are the examples he would find in the three Latin poets he most admired: Virgil, Statius, Claudian. The temple of Juno built by Dido is described by Virgil in a notable passage (*Aen.* i. 446 ff.)—a passage Chaucer would be bound to ponder as he prepared the version of Aeneas's story that is shortly to be introduced. Virgil shows us Juno's temple as Aeneas saw it when his mother Venus left him in Carthage. Oxford's first professor of Poetry, Joseph Trapp, said of Virgil's account of the decoration of that temple and Juno's golden statue that 'there never was a finer picture of a picture than this'. The scenes of the Trojan War that adorn Juno's temple surely gave Chaucer the suggestion for depicting scenes from the *Aeneid* itself within *Venus's* temple. And a poet with *Fama* for his theme would not overlook lines like *bellaque iam fama totum vulgata per orbem* (*Aen.* i. 457)—'famus batellis vulgat throu the warld' as Gavin Douglas renders it—or the phrase in Aeneas's words to Achates: *feret haec aliquam tibi fama salutem* (463): 'wenys thou na this fame sall do thee gude?[1]'

Virgil, however, provides no account of a temple of Venus beyond the two lines describing her shrine at Paphos, whither she flies, 'cutting the clouds', from Carthage:

> ubi templum illi centumque Sabaeo
> Ture calent arae sertisque recentibus halant.
>
> (Aen. i. 416–17)
>
> (Qhairin thar doith ane hundreth altaris stand,
> Hait byrning full of Saber sens all houris
> And smellyng sweit with fresch garlandis of flouris.)

Brief as it is, this description of Virgil's coloured most subsequent *ecphrases* of temples honouring the goddess of love, and not least those in Statius (*Sylvae*, I. ii. 144–56) and in Claudian (*Epithalamium Honorii*, 85 ff.).[2] That these were well known in the fourteenth century can be shown from adaptations of the first by Boccaccio (in his *Teseida*) and of the second by Chaucer himself, who sifted it for phrases applicable to the Temple of Venus as presented in the *Parliament*.[3] From Claudian the theme was

---

[1] Renderings of the Aeneid are from Douglas's *Eneados* except where otherwise noted.

[2] The later association of Venus with Paphos was determined by this reference in *Aen.* i: cf. Isidore of Seville, *Lib. Etym.* VIII. xi. 2, XIV. vi. 14, and Guido delle Colonne, *Historia Destructionis Troiæ*, x. Servius's commentary on the passage dwells on *ture* and *sertis*. Hence in Boccaccio's *Teseida* as in the Knight's Tale (*CT*, A. 1961) Venus in her temple has 'a rose gerlande, fressh and wel smellynge'. See p. 18 below.

[3] See Bennett, *Parlement of Foules*, pp. 79 n. 1, 89 n. 1, 119 n. 2.

taken over in the fifth century by Sidonius Apollinaris (*Carmen*, xi. 15) and from Sidonius by Alanus of Lille in the *Anticlaudianus* that we shall later find Chaucer recalling in another context (986). Alain's intent, however, was to honour Nature, not Venus, and his account of her pillared and pictorial palace concerns us here only as showing how the set description of a hall or temple dedicated to a deity had become a medium for moral and philosophical truths—a development quite distinct from the pictures of wondrous palaces and stately pleasure-domes of early French romance (such as the 'salle des images' in Thomas's *Tristan* or the faery palace in *Guinga-mor*). It was a development that Spenser was to continue in one direction with his Bower of Bliss and House of Tempe, and Polifilo in another—his *Hypnerotomachia* included actual pictures of such halls and temples. When Boccaccio came to describe a temple of Venus in the stanzas that Chaucer transferred from the *Teseida* to the *Parliament* his commentary on those stanzas showed the influence of Alain's allegory. Thus he allegorizes the temple's brassy columns as expressing the strength of love. By the same token, if the temple in *Fame* is 'ymad of glas' (120) it is to denote—as any renaissance iconologist would recognize—love's insubstantiality.[1] We should therefore be the less surprised if 360 lines later this temple vanishes like a phantom—or if, still later, the house of fickle Fame is built on ice (and the home of Rumour made of brittle twigs).

But before considering what significance we are to attach to the architectural details of Chaucer's temple we must

---

[1] Cf. (e.g.) Cesare Ripa's *Iconologia* (1613), cit. Erwin Panofsky, *Studies in Iconology* (1939), 1962 ed., p. 162, n. 114: 'glass signifies by its fragility the vanity of all things on earth.' *Vitrei amici vitro sunt donandi* (Taylor, *The Proverb*, p. 68) was a commonplace.

note its likeness to a temple mentioned in a source undoubtedly familiar to him and cited later (1469 ff.) as an
authority for the very story that is the groundwork of
Virgil's epic. For the Middle Ages the 'matter of Troy' was
essentially the narrative set down in the thirteenth century
by Guido delle Colonne; and for Guido a temple of
Venus, located on a known and named island, was the
setting for the rape of Helen by Paris that occasioned the
launching of the thousand ships and at last the burning
of the towers of Ilium:

> Erat autem in hec insula Cytharea quoddam templum in
> honorem Veneris *ex antiquo constructum*, mire pulchritudinis, et
> diviciis multum plenum . . .[1]

So Guido's account of Paris's enamourment begins; and
Chaucer's mention of 'figures of olde werke' (126-7), with
his insistence on the art and richness displayed in the
temple of his dream, suggests that he had Guido before
him as he wrote. Visionary as his temple is, and 'un-
classical' as its Venus will prove to be, Chaucer had
strong reason, as we shall see, for presenting everything
pertaining to the Troy story as historical and so for con-
sulting Guido, the accredited source of it.

Three features of Venus's temple require closer scrutiny:

1. Its interior structure and design. Brief though the
references to these are, they leave no doubt that it resembled
less a classical temple than a Gothic church of the late
decorated or early perpendicular period when stained glass
was at its richest and stone grew plastic in the hands of the
sculptors of the Percy tomb at Beverley or the carvers of

---

[1] *Historia Destructionis Troiæ*, vii (ed. N. E. Griffin, Cambridge, Mass.,
1936, p. 69); for Lydgate's version of the passage see his *Troy Book*, II. 3435 ff.
Boccaccio's statue of Venus that in the *Teseida* (cf. *CT*, A. 2265-8) makes
answer to prayer, apparently derives from Guido.

the pillars at Strassburg; and a 'chirche' is what Chaucer later calls it (473). To search for an exact counterpart in fourteenth-century architecture would be to ignore the element of the marvellous in dream-poetry. But one master-piece in the new style must have caught and pleased the eye of the poet who became Clerk of the King's Works: namely is the chapel of St. Stephen at Westminster, now destroyed. Of its ornament one who saw it when it was uncovered in 1795 said 'the sculpture, painting, and guilding dazzled the eye of vision'; which is precisely the effect Chaucer intends to convey here. 'Ymad of glas' is the only clue he gives as to the exterior appearance of the temple. The phrase would be apt enough for the window-walls that the new perpendicular style made possible, though it might be hard to point to any striking example of these known to Chaucer except the East window of Gloucester cathedral; and the words perhaps mean no more than that 'with glas Were al the windows wel yglased Ful clere' as in the *Book of the Duchess*, where the windows offer room for the stories of both Troy and Rome (326–31), with much else besides.

2. The murals illustrating the tale of Aeneas. The art of mural painting, either on stone or on panels of wood, reached its peak in Chaucer's lifetime, and again St. Ste-phen's chapel provides—or rather provided—the supreme examples. The poet describes the scenes from the tale at one point as 'peynted' (211) but usually as 'grave' (157, 253, 256, 451)—terms not necessarily contradictory; they allow the surmise that he had in mind genuine classical remains (marble chests or altars showing carved subjects and traces of colour, such as he might have seen in Italy); and 'graven images' (472–3) certainly seems to imply some kind of bas-relief. Yet such was the sophistication

of the St. Stephen's painters that—to judge from one surviving panel—they could provide the illusion of such carving without resort to the chisel; and heavy gilding, the incising of outlines, raised ornament in *gesso sottile*, Master Hugh of St. Albans' experiment in glazing with colour to give the effect of a receding floor—all this was diminishing the differences between painting and sculpture in Chaucer's day, and we need not wonder if he appears to forget them.[1]

For mural decoration whether in paint or tapestry the tale of Troy had long been, and long continued, a favourite sub⁄ject. No classical or early medieval example survives, but for our purpose literary evidence will suffice, and it can be found in the thirteenth⁄century romance of *King Alysaunder* in which Queen Candace, when infatuated with Alexander

> led hym to chaumbres of nobleys
> þere he dude of his harneys;
> Of Troye was þereinne al þe story,
> Hou Gregeis hadden þe victory.   (7656–9)

The architectural setting in that romance is almost as wondrous as the temple of Venus in *Fame*:

> þe bemes þereinne weren of bras,
> þe wyndewes of riche glas,
> þe pynnes [pinnacles] weren of yvory.   (7658–60)

But the pictures are presumably intended to appeal to Alexander's *martial* spirit, as the rich materials would to

---

[1] For an account of the St. Stephen's murals see E. W. Tristram, *English Wall Painting of the Fourteenth Century* (1955), pp. 46, 58 (and 206–19). Their re⁄discovery marked an important stage in the medieval revival fostered by Smirke and 'Antiquity' Smith: see *Bulletin of the Metropolitan Museum*, New York, March 1962. They were partly destroyed by the fire of 1834, partly by Wyatt a few years later.

Chaucer is almost the first to use *grave* of sculpture; cf. *M.E.D.*, s.v.

his sense of the luxurious. The resemblance to Chaucer's building is thus merely superficial. More pertinent is Chrétien de Troye's account of the whole story of the *Aeneid* embroidered on a saddle, in his *Erec* (5338 ff.):

> S'i fu antailliee l'estoire
> Comant Eneas vint de Troie,
> Comant a Cartaige, a grant joie,
> Dido en son lev le reçut,
> Comant Eneas la deçut;
> Comant ele por lui s'ocist;
> Comant Eneas puis conquist
> Laurente et tote Lonbardie
> Dom il fu rois tote sa vie.

The *Aeneid*, then, was a likely artistic source even in Chrétien's time, and Aeneas was already established in the role of deceiver. But from Chrétien we can learn nothing further.

3. The 'figure' of Venus and her attendant deities 'in portreyture' (131). It is hardly clear—and it hardly matters—whether these are to be envisaged as painted merely, or carved. Elsewhere (in the Knight's Tale) Chaucer distinguished between a 'portretour' and a 'kervere of images'; but a temple seems to require a statue, such as the golden image to be seen in Gozzoli's panel, now in the National Gallery, showing Helen's rape; and the figure in the oratory of Venus described in the Knight's Tale (*CT*, A. 1918 ff.) is beyond question a statue. The attendant figures, however, are there painted 'on the wal'; so we should perhaps think of the statue of Venus here as in a similar niche, with her doves, Cupid, and Vulcan painted on the wall of the niche. Like that in the Knight's Tale, it might be patterned with 'wawes grene and brighte as any glas'—the sea being Venus's native element.

The description of Venus herself so strikingly resembles
that in the Knight's Tale (*C T*, A. 1955 ff.)—not to mention again the Venus transferred from Boccaccio's *Teseida*
to the *Parliament*—as to suggest that Chaucer found in the
iconography of this goddess a particular fascination. For
such an interest he had precedent both recent and respectable. Early in the fourteenth century the Latin writings
of the mythographers whom Boccaccio was later to rifle
for *De Genealogia Deorum* had attracted the attention of
certain learned English friars. One of them, John Ridevall,
had succeeded in converting the fifth-century *Mythologiae*
of Fulgentius into a preacher's handbook, with the pagan
gods standing for the several virtues. How easily the
preacher's handbook might become a painter's may be
judged from Ridevall's name for his descriptions of the
gods—(*poetica*) *pictura*[1]—and Chaucer seems to have
responded to the pictorial suggestion, whether he found
it in Fulgentius, in Ridevall's *Fulgencius metaforalis*, or in
Ridevall's French Benedictine contemporary Pierre Bersuire. Before moralizing Ovid's *Metamorphoses* Bersuire
had found it desirable to provide what he called pictures
of Ovid's divinities, and he drew not only on Fulgentius
and his successors, but on the *Africa* of 'the venerable
Master Francesco Petrarca'—a work which likewise contains what Petrarch calls *species deorum* (and likewise leaves
it unclear whether these are wall-paintings or gilded
bas-reliefs).

[1] See Beryl Smalley, *English Friars and Antiquity in the early fourteenth century*
(Oxford, 1960), pp. 261–4. But miniaturists would have studied such passages
before Chaucer did. He probably knew illuminated manuscripts showing the
influence of these prescriptions: the fifteenth-century French manuscript of the
Histoire de la destruction de Troie which presents a naked Venus in a fantastical
temple (see *Manuscrits à Peintures du xiiie au xvie siècle*, pl. 36) doubtless had an
earlier exemplar.

The attraction of this mythographical tradition for Chaucer results in a Venus very different from the divinity he had found described in the *Roman de la Rose*, who was 'arayed richely' with robe, brooch, girdle, and 'tresour' and bore in her right hand 'Of brennyng fyr a blasyng brond' (*Rom*, 3705–22). Bersuire's Venus, like the statue in this temple, and in Theseus's, is 'naked fletinge in a see' and Bersuire tells us why, in all the decency of a learned language, and by a surprising resort to Isaiah:

Est nuda quia vix homo eam celat vixque potest esse qui appareat. Et in mari, id est delitiarum opulentia vult natare. . . . Venus etiam in mari fingitur genita pro eo quod luxuria ab opulentia et a delitiarum fluxibus non recedit; unde nudam meretricem videtur alloqui scriptura:

Esa 23 [vv. 10 and 16]: *transi terram tuam quasi flumen, filia maris*; et sequitur: *Sume citharam, circui civitatem, meretrix oblivioni tradita*, etc. [See additional note, p. 188.]

That the pagan embodiment of female beauty should become in Christian eyes a symbol of carnal pleasure is hardly surprising. But that she could be something different from mere sensuality we learn from Boccaccio, and at the very point where he presents her in her most alluring posture—recumbent, and adorned only with a zone that reveals as much as it conceals (*Teseida*, vii. 65). In his own commentary on this passage in the *Teseida* Boccaccio takes occasion to distinguish (as to be sure others had done) between the Venus who smiles on marriage, the Venus who incites to love *paramour*, and the Venus of unchastity. It may seem that Boccaccio here as elsewhere is trying to have the best of both worlds. But undoubtedly Venus's nudity did not in itself denote wantonness: for one thing, the astrological Venus was often depicted as nude—as in an illustration of Chaucer's own *Complaint of Mars* (in the Fairfax MS. that contains *Fame* itself) and in the fifteenth-century Estense *De Sphaera*.[1]

Up to this point, then, Chaucer's account of the goddess would not justify us in equating her with the *meretrix* or harlot of the moralizers. Its very brevity, how-ever, suggests that the few additional details pertaining to her are not set down at random. In fact they too show the influence of fourteenth-century mythological learning. The fragrance that pervaded Venus's Paphian temple (in Virgil) had long since been associated with roses; most of the mythographers had given Venus a 'rose garlond whyt and reed' (135), as do the Dominican Hopeman, the miniaturist of Fairfax 16, the Estense artist, and others. Working on a larger canvas in the Knight's Tale, Chaucer will add that the roses were 'fressh and wel smellynge' (*CT*, A. 1961)—as if newly provided by one of the goddess's supplicants. The association of roses and *amor* hardly needs documenting.[2] Equally traditional are the doves, which we may think of as flickering round Venus's head, as they do in the Knight's Tale, though Lydgate, elaborat-ing the scene in his *Temple of Glass* (541) will represent them as offered by Venus's worshippers.[3] Again the amorous suggestion is plain, at least to any reader of the *Parliament* (ll. 237–8) or of Boccaccio's gloss on *Teseida*, vii. 57.

But in *Fame* the doves share the line and the alliteration with 'daun Cupido' (137). The brief allusion implies that

[1] At Modena: see *Il 'de Sphaera, estense e l'iconografia astrologica*, S. Samek Ludovici (Milan, 1958), tav. 10. For the Fairfax miniature see p. 23, n. 1.

[2] But D. W. Robertson, jr., has assembled examples: *A Preface to Chaucer* (Princeton, 1963), pp. 95 f.

[3] In his *Troy Book* (ii. 5712–33) he adds sparrows to the doves.

he is to play no major role. 'Daun' is only slightly honorific when compared with the Cupid who is 'lord and sire' or 'our lord' in the *Parliament* (12, 212) or 'the mighty god of love' whose golden hair was haloed by the sun and whose face shone so fiercely 'that wel unnethes myghte I him beholde' (*LGW*, F. 230 ff.). Omitting now the usual reference to his wings and arrows, Chaucer adds only that he is blind. Though *Caecus est amor* was an ancient and familiar commonplace, it was not one that sorted with the god's character as Guillaume de Lorris had conceived it: in the *Roman* Cupid is of such heavenly beauty and imperious aspect that

> he can cherles daunten, he,
> And maken folkes pryde fallen.
> And he can wel these lordes thrallen;
>
> .   .   .   .
>
> He seemed as he were an aungel
> That doun were comen fro hevene clere.
>
> (*Rom*, 880–2, 916–17);

hence his angelic wings and forbidding glance in the *Legend*, though in one detail Chaucer there deliberately departs from tradition:

> And al be that men seyn that blind is he,
> Algate me thoughte wel he mighte ysee;
> For sternely on me he gan biholde,
> So that his loking doth myn herte colde.
>
> (*LGW*, F. 169–72)

The traditional blindness is presumably no more than a material figuring of his lack of respect for rank or person. But once so figured it could be rationalized in a quite different sense—and was, by Bersuire and by Boccaccio, whose *De Genealogia Deorum* summarizes the doctrine:

Love is blindfold, says Boccaccio, 'ut advertamus amantes ignorare quo tendant, nulla eorum esse judicia, nulle rerum distinctiones sed sola passione duci . . .' (IX. c. 4. 95c).

Gower will read this irrationality into classical legend:

> So whan thei [sc. Cupid and Venus] weren bothe al one,
> As he which yhen hadde none
> To se reson, his moder kiste;
> And sche also, that nothing wiste
> Bot that which unto lust [desire] belongeth,
> To ben hire love him underfongeth.
> Thus was he blinde, and sche unwys;
>
> (*Confessio Amantis*, v. 1411–17)

But equally relevant is the unfavourable comparison that Bersuire makes between this irrational, indifferent (and hence sinister) Cupid, and that other pagan deity *Fortuna*, who often shares this blindness—and is to share it also, in so far as it denotes perverse unreason, with *Fama*. Thus, as Venus with her wilful Cupid is to be one pole of reference in the poem, it is wholly fitting that perverse 'Fame' (who will, like Venus, have subordinate attendants in a splendid building) should be the other.

Alongside Cupid stands Vulcan 'that in his face was ful broun' (139). Thanks to Ovid, Vulcan's relations with Venus were familiar enough to be merely alluded to (as in the Knight's Tale (*CT*, A. 2389) and *Teseida* (vii. 25, 38)) rather than retold; and we can distinguish Chaucer's Arcite from his Palamon in that tale according to their different references to the divine pair. Palamon, praying in Venus's oratory for success in love, names her first as 'Doughter to Jove and spouse of Vulcanus'; Arcite, praying to Mars, implores him to remember the pain *he* had suffered in his adulterous love for Venus which brought him into Vulcan's net. Not that medieval writers or commentators ever sympathize with the wronged husband. For Gower (*CA*, v. 646–7, and gloss) as for Jean de Meun, 'lothly and malgracious' Vulcan is a jealous 'schrewe', Venus a *mal mariée* cumbered by an old and ugly smith. 'Swart' and 'smotry' are Lydgate's epithets for him (*Troy Book*, ii. 5803) and they reflect the same lines of de Meun's that led Chaucer to make Vulcan 'brown' of face:

> Car Vulcanus si laiz estait,
> Et si *charbonez* de sa forge,
> Pars mains et *par vis* e par gorge,
> Que pour riens Venus l'amast,
> Combien que mari le clamast.
> (*Rom*, 13864–8; La Vieille *loq.*)

He was so ugly, in short, that Venus couldn't bring herself to love him however much he claimed her as his wife. Practically the only exception to this view of Vulcan is found in the 'Third Vatican mythographer', who cites Remigius's convenient distinction between the two Venuses: one 'voluptuaria libidinum dea', whose son is said to be Hermaphroditus; the other 'casta et pudica, quam honestis praeesse amoribus *quamque Vulcani* [*dicit*] *uxorem*'. The latter Venus, virtuous and modest, represents wisdom and the other virtues. John Scotus Eriugena (who has room for a third Venus, *procreatrix*) repeats this distinc' tion.[1] But it did nothing to improve Vulcan's reputation, even among the Christian moralizers of Ovid, who regularly interpret the story as a warning against inequality in marriage (thus Bersuire and the fifteenth'century prose *Ovide Moralisé*) or see in Vulcan's forge the fires of lust.

---

[1] In his commentary on Martianus Capella's *De Nuptiis Mercurii et Philologiae* (cit. *Speculum*, xxxi (1956), 667).

Nothing in Chaucer's actual words commits him to
a view of Vulcan as moral or immoral, as respectable or
as ridiculous. None the less his description, following hard
on the reference to a blind Cupid, helps in its context—
even if we read 'brown' as a gently humorous euphemism
—to modify the initial impression of the temple as a place
of unalloyed beauty and delight. Not so startling as the
appearance in the *Parliament* (in the same setting) of the
god Priapus 'in swich aray as whan the asse him shente ...'
(255–6), it has its own slightly disturbing effect. Never
does Chaucer present a temple of Venus which is wholly
beautiful within. That in the Knight's Tale, like that in
the *Parliament*, is the place of tears, sighs, and lamentation;
both are decorated with the stories of woebegone or foolish
lovers; among these in the *Parliament* being the Dido who
is shortly to be presented in *Fame*.

We are now in a better position to see how far Chaucer
is from re-creating a classical temple of Venus and how
closely he conforms to the pattern of moralizing mythographers and commentators. The Copenhagen text of the
fourteenth-century *Ovide Moralisé* (and probably other
manuscripts now lost) begins with an account of the chief
divinities mentioned in Ovid's work 'tant par figures
comme par escriptures y adjoustez par le commentateur'.
Amongst them, of course, is 'La figure de Venus et
comment elle dost estre painte'. The miniaturist of the
Fairfax MS. might be following these instructions almost
to the letter; and they conveniently include all the attributes
and attendants that Chaucer gives this goddess in *Fame*,
or elsewhere:

. . . She must be painted in the form of a very beautiful
maiden swimming in the sea, holding in her hand 'une lamine
d'ardoise' [? a mirror], surrounded by roses and flowers, and

above her head doves flying about; and she must be assigned
in marriage to Vulcan, god of fire, very ugly and deformed.
In front of her must be three young naked girls called the Three
Graces, two with faces turned towards her, one with her back
to her. Near her must be her winged son Cupid, but he must
be blind, and shooting an arrow at Apollo from the bow he
is holding (because of which the gods were much troubled and
the child in panic fled to hide himself near his mother). . .[1]

There follows first the 'literal' exposition: Venus is
painted as a naked girl because she is feminine; she is
shown married to Vulcan because she is warm, and
floating on the sea because she is moist; and she is said to
have conceived Cupid, i.e. the concupiscence of the flesh,
because she arouses concupiscence. Then comes the moral
exposition derived from Fulgentius, according to whom
she represents the voluptuous life and swims because she
wishes to be continually surrounded with delights. The
object in her hand (usually a cittern) represents joy and
merriment. The three Graces may be *either* luxury, pride,
and avarice *or* (Fulgentius is as accommodating as are
interpreters of Melville's White Whale) faith, hope, and
charity. Cupid is winged to show that carnal love is
sudden and headstrong, and blind because it is wilful and
also because all who adhere to *folle amour* are blind: as
Seneca says, *Amor judicium nescit*; which is why the old
poets wanted Cupid to be painted blind, like Fortune.
The more love struggles to get free the more it is engaged,
like Narcissus who fatally loved his own reflection. Thus
a poor man in love with a high-born lady will doom

---

[1] The French text was published by C. De Boer, *Ovid Moralisé*, Tome V
(Amsterdam, 1938), p. 402, the Fairfax miniature by Fritz Saxl and Hans
Meier, *Catalogue of astrological and mythological illuminated manuscripts* (London,
1953), iii. 2, Tafel VI, Abb. 18.

himself and her to shame. Fortune also, just as if she were blind, suddenly elevates poor men and throws the noble and worthy into poverty and disgrace.

The differences between this exegesis and Boccaccio's will suggest several possible reasons for Chaucer's reticence about the Venus he depicts in this poem. But stronger than any logical cause must have been his instinct for avoiding a *moralitas* when a more cogent effect could be obtained by poetic placing and proportioning; when, in short, he could trust the tale of Dido and Aeneas as it will be found figured in Venus's temple, to show the many-sidedness of love (including connubial love); and when he could so pattern his poem as to bring out and remind us (much later) of Vulcan's banausic role by balancing against him Fame's emissary Aeolus, god of winds, with whom Virgil memorably associates him in the *Aeneid* (viii. 416 ff.) as the maker of Aeneas's shield. Chaucer's summary treat-ment of Aeneas's story as pictured in the temple will allow no mention of that scene; but the very presence of the smith in Venus's company subtly prepares us for the introduction of other themes besides the purely amorous. We need not, then, read into these figures anticipations of a classical revival or the neoplatonic symbolism of later Florentines. And in fact Chaucer quickly diverts our gaze from them to the story in which they will be overshadowed by Jupiter, and the chief roles will be played by mortals.

What this story is to be we divine at once from the first mural inscription that catches the dreamer's eye, rendering as it does (143–8) the famous opening lines of *Aeneid*, i. And once directed to the *Aeneid* we can see that Venus and her temple 'belong' to that poem in a very special way, and that to decorate its walls with scenes from Virgil's epic was in no sense an afterthought of the poet. It was

Venus who inspired the initial action of the *Aeneid*, and summary as Chaucer's version of the story is, he will omit none of her significant appearances in it. Though he says nothing of her actual flight to her Cyprian temple (*Aen.* i. 416–17), he can hardly have ignored the description of that temple from which, as we have seen, his own account in the *Parliament* ultimately derives. The rigorous economy of this opening book allows no room either for Juno's temple (in which Aeneas beheld his own past history as in a mirror that could recapture time) or for Apollo's temple at Cumae (*Aen.* vi. 14–34) with its doors displaying the histories of the Minotaur ('*Veneris* monimenta nefandae'), Daedalus, and Icarus—though Chaucer will have occasion to refer to these much later in very unVirgilian contexts. But the vividness with which Virgil evokes the scenes depicted in Juno's temple doubtless prompted Chaucer to describe Venus's temple as similarly historiated, and, taking a hint from the technique of those twenty lines in *Aeneid*, vi, to present the story of Troy and Aeneas obliquely in a series of scenes such as might be accommodated on separate panels. And as Aeneas is represented as admiring in the temples of Carthage and of Cumae masterpieces that were modern rather than antique, so Chaucer puts these scenes or panels in a 'contemporary gothic' church. When Marlowe, writing *Hero and Leander*, came to enlarge on Musaeus's reference to a temple and to describe its mythological decorations, he used the same term: 'So faire a church as this, had Venus none.'

But, quite apart from the significance of the setting of the pictures in Venus's temple, the Aeneasepic with its episodes is also both formally and thematically related to the main development of the English poem. The relation is not unlike that of a digression from the central action in

an *epyllion*; and if we take Shakespeare's *Rape of Lucrece*
as an example of this genre the scene in which Lucrece
ponders the painted cloth setting forth the same tale of
Troy will provide an analogy. The painting hints
obliquely at the Hecuba-like role that Lucrece must
soon play:

> To this well painted peece is Lucrece come,
> To find a place where all distress is steld,
> Many she sees, where cares have carved some,
> But none where all distress and dolor dweld
> Till she dispayring Hecuba beheld
>
> . . . .
>
> In her the Painter had anatomis'd
> Times ruine, beauties wracke and grim cares raign;
>
> (1443-7; 1450-1)

And Lucrece's comment on the *casus belli*, Helen's rape—
it serves to return us to the central story as it shortly un-
folds—is precisely what Dido's complaint will be:

> Why should the private pleasure of some one
> Become the public plague of manie mo?
>
> (1478-9)

Even so the plight of Dido, which Chaucer makes the
high point of Virgil's story, will serve obliquely to
introduce the twin themes of the rest of the poem: the
nature of 'Fame' and the search for tidings of 'Loves
folke'. At the same time the content of this classical tale
provides that element of contrast and variety which is
characteristic of good Gothic art in general and of
Chaucer's in particular.

Though the opening of the new *descriptio* is signalized
by a close rendering of *Aeneid*, i. 1-4, the poet nowhere
claims that he is viewing the story, the whole story, and

nothing but the story of Virgil's epic. Thanks to Virgil's prestige, that story had been retold, abbreviated, and adapted in a dozen different ways before Chaucer's time, and his first readers would owe their knowledge of it as often to these *remaniements* as to the original poem—just as many a modern reader 'knows' Malory without ever having seen Caxton's or Vinaver's text. The synoptic process had begun, in a sense, with Ovid (*Metamorphoses*, xiv) and Chaucer may well have read Ovid's epitome of Virgil long before opening Virgil. Of medieval recensions two may be taken as typical—both made as early as the twelfth century:

(i) The *Ilias Latina* of the Victorine canon Chèvre d'Or (Simon Aurea Lapsa), which is more than its title suggests and which survives in two versions. The longer of these has been claimed as providing Chaucer with authority for placing Venus's prayer to Jupiter in the new context that he gives it at l. 215.[1] However this may be, it certainly could not be claimed that Chaucer learnt from the *Ilias* anything of the art of condensation: the first sixty lines of his version correspond to some 520 in Chèvre d'Or's.

(ii) The anonymous *Roman d'Énéas* (*c.* 1160; *c.* 10,000 ll.). This poem would be more worthy of Chaucer's attention, and not only because it was the first vernacular retelling of the story; it has some poetic merits of its own and it shows a certain freedom in re-ordering (and deleting) events and characters. This is essentially the *Aeneid* as the Middle Ages (and Chaucer) saw it: a romance, with Dido as its heroine. Thus and only thus does Virgil come

---

[1] See Albert C. Friend in *Speculum*, xxviii (1953), 317–23. Andrea Lancia's fourteenth-century Tuscan *La Istoria di Eneas*, ed. G. Folena (Palermo, 1956), also gave the main outlines of Virgil's story: cf. *Medieval Studies* (Toronto), xxv (1963), 148.

within the compass of the authors of the *Roman de la Rose*; and even Dante, reading Virgil with fresh eyes, alludes in the *Commedia* more often to *Aeneid*, iv (Dido's book) than to any other.[1] That Chaucer read the *Roman d'Énéas* one cannot establish; but he would certainly have relished and approved its treatment of the central figures.

Chaucer's selection of incidents is such as always to show Aeneas under Venus's aegis: a 'romantic' approach that persisted (to Gavin Douglas's disgust) up to the time of Caxton and the French exemplar for Caxton's so-called *Eneydos*. The hero's long account of his woes and wanderings (occupying part of the second and all of Virgil's third book) Chaucer reduces to some thirty-five lines and begins, significantly enough, with Venus's appearance to 'her sone' (162–5; cf. *Aen*. ii. 589–620). But what Chaucer here omits he does not necessarily forget. Thus, though he here passes lightly over 'the matter of Troy', its siege and ruin, he will later (1467–74) introduce the writers whose names had become synonymous with it. Again, the early account of Aeolus, his country and his operations (in *Aen*. i. 50 ff.) will contribute much to the action in Fame's hall (1571–1601). Chaucer nowhere actually mentions the prelude to Aeneas's narrative—that striking scene in which Iopas hymns to a regal Dido, as yet hardly disturbed by passion, the wonders of creation:

> Cithara crinitus Iopas
> personat aurata, docuit quem maximus Atlas.

---

[1] See *Rom.* 13173–210. Dido's suicide is a constant item in illustrations of the manuscripts and early printed editions of that poem. Dante (who has in all some forty references to the *Aeneid*) cites or refers to *Aen*. iv some six times (e.g. *Purg*. xxx. 48: cf. *Aen*. iv. 23). Chaucer, exploring Dante at the time that he was meditating on the *Aeneid*, would be alert to these allusions and would find in them precedent for his own devotion to the 'anima cortese Mantovana'.

hic canit errantem lunam solisque labores,
unde hominum genus et pecudes, unde imber et ignes,
Arcturum, pluviasque Hyades, geminosque Triones;
Quid tantum Oceano properent se tinguere soles
hiberni, vel quae tardis mora noctibus obstet . . .

(*Aen.* i. 740–6)

(Quhairof mankynd is maid he schew ful plaine,
Quhairof bestis, and quhat engendrys rayn,
Quhairof cummys thundir and fyry levin . . .)

So one cannot prove that he felt the contrast between the
serene objectivity of this passage and the painful introspec-
tion to which Dido is prey when next we see her. But it
may not be a coincidence that he will provide a similar
contrast, if on a larger scale and in different sequence. For
the first solace offered to him as a dreamer oppressed by the
woes of Dido and of all lovers will be a revelation of the
same natural wonders that Iopas had sung to his lyre:

. . . the eyrish bestes,
Cloudes, mistes and tempestes,
Snowes, hailes, reines, windes,
And the engendring in hir kindes.

(*HF*, 965–8)

Iopas's poem and his golden lyre make him a disciple of
Apollo, whom Chaucer will in due course invoke (1091–
1109). He has reversed the Virgilian sequence and put the
poetry of Dido's woes before the *mirabilia mundi*.

Like most medieval redactors of Virgil, Chaucer constructs what they would have called a *narratio naturalis*
out of Virgil's *narratio artificialis*: that is, he rearranges the
events in their chronological sequence.[1] And within the
framework of the events that he selects for his synopsis
of the *Aeneid* he allows himself certain extensions and

---

[1] Cf. *Medieval Studies* (Toronto), xxiv (1964), 238.

embellishments. Thus his description of Creusa, Aeneas's wife, 'Which that he lovede as his lyf' (176), intensifies the *O dulcis conjunx* of *Aeneid*, ii. 777; and he seizes a hint in these closing lines of the second book (*non haec sine numine divum Eveniunt*: ('Without the powers divine these things are not disposed', 777–8) to find a place (in l. 188) for that notion of Destiny which he must needs ignore when retelling *Aeneid*, iv (where it is *Aeneas* who is pre⁄sented as subject to Destiny), since he would have our sympathy for Dido to be unreserved. Again, he underlines the blame to be attached to Juno, Venus's rival, by his sudden swerve into direct address:

> Ther saw I thee, cruel Juno,
> That art daun Iupiteres wyf
> That hast yhated, al thy lyf,
> Al the Troianysshe blood,
> Renne and cry, *as thou were wood*,
> On Eolus, the god of windes . . .   (198–203)

This characterization is partly justified by Virgil's account of Juno's behaviour at the judgement of Paris, noted at the very outset of the *Aeneid*.[1] But her frenzy, like her insistence that every single Trojan should perish (205 f.), is a heightening added by a poet who takes the Trojan disaster to heart; for as a citizen of *Troy novaunt* Chaucer naturally identifies himself with the Trojan wanderers, and writes as if he too were victim of the goddess's malice. So did the 'English Gaufride' whom he is to honour later as 'bearer up of Troy' (1472)—a reference that helps to explain this expenditure of lines on Juno, and to tie the themes of this first book to those of the third. In the third

---

[1] *Aen.* i. 4, 28, 47. Chaucer has perhaps been influenced by Virgil's account of the way in which Dido (favoured by Juno) later behaves: cf. *Aen.* iv. 300–1 (*saevit inops animi totamque incensa per urbem Bacchatur*), and 469 (*veluti demens*).

book, too, Fame herself will display something like Juno's impetuosity, and like her will treat the god of winds as her menial (1623 etc.).

The violence of this address to Juno, and the ensuing tempest, bring out by contrast the tenderness of the next allusion to her rival—'Venus . . . *ye, my lady* dere' (213); it is just such a phrase of affectionate respect as those ardent lovers of the Invocation (85 ff.) might use. This open avowal of the poet's is sufficient, in terms of literary dream-psychology at least, to explain why he dreamt of Venus's temple. It binds the self-revelatory poet of the Proem into the initial pattern of the poem proper. And it is as Venus's poet, we might say, that he now takes it on himself to make certain adjustments to the epic machinery. We do not find Virgil's Venus begging Jove to save the Trojan fleet (214 ff.), for Virgil does not introduce her till the storm has ceased. Her tears (*tristior et lacrimis oculos suffusa nitentis*, i. 228: 'All dolorus hir eyn full of bricht teris') are then tears of pity at Aeneas's plight, shipwrecked as he is on the coast of Africa; and in Virgil Jove's part is not to still the storm but to confirm the happy destiny of her lineage:

> Parce metu, Cytherea, manent immota tuorum
> fata tibi.   (*Aen.* i. 257–8)

It is impertinent to suggest, as is sometimes done, that Chaucer's change or rather conflation here arises from his misreading of the text: following the ancient precedent of Dares and Dictys, not to mention the *Roman d'Énéas*, he has introduced a new scene, and one so congenial to him that he will re-stage it, though in a completely different setting, in *The Canterbury Tales*.[1] And this

[1] See *CT*, A. 2438–42, where Jupiter is busy to *stente* (cf. *Fame*, 221) the strife between Mars and Venus, who later (ibid. 2665) weeps, as here, lest another of her knights (Palamon) should be vanquished.

Jupiter, stiller of storms, *hominum sator atque deorum*, is to have a similar controlling part in the main action of our poem: the poet-dreamer himself is in the second part to witness and experience his benevolent power.

Having landed at Carthage, Aeneas the next day meets his divine mother in the forest, wearing what Joseph Trapp called 'a lovely Romantick Dress':

> Venatrix dederatque comas diffundere ventis,
> Nuda genu, nodoque sinus collecta fluentis.
>
> (*Aen.* i. 319-20)

Chaucer ignores this indication that her skirt is kirtled 'a little abune the kne', just as he ignores Deguilleville's moralizing on her 'venerye' (see Lydgate's rendering of the *Pelèrinage de la vie humaine*, 8130-80), but he finds room in his rendering of the lines to hint that as a huntress Venus is acting a part:

> . . . goinge in a queynt aray
> As she had ben an hunteresse
> With wind blowinge upon her tresse   (228-30)

'As she had ben . . .' evidently derives from the gloss *quasi venatrix* ('huntress-like') in the sixth-century commentary of Servius, which regularly accompanied medieval texts of Virgil. The wind that waves her tresses was later to stir the ringlets of Botticelli's wave-borne Venus; and in Botticelli's day, if not in Chaucer's, hair loosely flowing like this would denote *voluptas*; at the least it gives us a picture of a vivid panel on the temple-wall reflecting, so to say, the graceful beauty of its central figure.

Chaucer (like Virgil) is careful to indicate that it was wholly through Venus's contriving that Dido became enamoured of Aeneas (240 f.). Yet Chaucer's Dido is not altogether Virgil's. Here are none of the 'green wounds' of love, none of the tortured confessions that make the opening of *Aeneid*, iv, so painful. She acts not only in good faith, but as if in obedience to Aeneas's entreaty: she

> Becam his love and leet him do
> Al that wedding longeth to. (243–4)

At this point Chaucer temporarily abandons both the Virgilian sequence of events (jumping from *Aeneid*, i, to *Aeneid*, iv) and the pictorial method, and deftly takes the occasion to establish his *persona* a little more firmly as one confessedly incapable of divining mysteries (Proem 15) and ignorant of the 'faculte' of love (249); it is thus that the eagle will later regard him (628, 866). Pictorial representation of the storm-bound lovers in itself offered no difficulty and in fact such pictures occur in manuscripts even from early medieval times; but Chaucer's deliberate refusal to say that this was wedlock *simpliciter* (244) indicates that his eye is fixed on his text, which here defies translation in medieval terms. Virgil regards this union for which *Tellus et pronuba Iuno* give the signal (iv. 166) as ominous and strange:

> fulsere ignes et conscius aether
> connubiis, summoque ululacunt vertice Nymphae.

(Of thar cuplyng wittering schew the ayr:
The flambe of fyreslaucht lychtnyt heir and thar;
And on the hillys hie toppis, but less,
Sat murnand nymphis . . .)

Connubium in the sense of civil wedlock (so at least Douglas interpreted it) is what Juno had designed:

> 'connubio iungam stabili propriamque dicabo.
> hic Hymenaeus erit.' (126–7)

('In sovir wedlok I sal conioyn hir thar
To be his propir spous for evirmair:
Apon this wyss thar wedding salbe wrocht.')

D

But that it was properly *conjugium*, lawful marriage, Virgil will not allow (hence, presumably, Douglas's derogatory 'cuplyng' above). Only Dido claims that it is:

> conjugium vocat: hoc praetexit nomine culpam. (172)
> (But clepys it spousage; and with that fayr name
> Clokyt and hyd hir cryme of oppyn shame.)

This suggestion of furtiveness and culpability the poet who was 'all women's friend' entirely suppresses not only here but in the *Legend of Good Women* where he depicts this saint of Cupid fleeing into the cave as if actively pursued by Aeneas—a suggestion hardly warranted by Virgil's

> speluncam Dido dux et Trojanus eandem
> deveniunt; (165–6)[1]

In *Fame* he avoids mention of Dido's emotions until he presents her as a victim of *fama*. And he is at pains to emphasize, even at the cost of seeming to turn back in his narrative course, that Dido treats the Trojan visitor as

> Hir lyf, hir love, hir lust [delight], hir lord; (258)

This is that lordship which the Franklin sees as the essence of true marriage (*CT*, F. 791–8). So Emelye loves her Palamon and the humble Griselda her Walter; and 'hir lyf' implies that 'unanimity', that identity of feeling which Orfeo so movingly asserts as he gazes on the fey Herodis:

> 'O leve liif, what is te?'[2]

---

[1] In *LGW*, F. 1230–3, Chaucer adds a new pathos to *ille dies primus leti primusque malorum Causa fuit* (169–70) by rendering it as 'This was the firste morwe Of hir gladnesse, and ginning of hir sorwe'; following a well-established scholiastic interpretation of *letum* ('death') which connected it etymologically with *læticia*: Ascensius (1462–1535) glosses *leti* as '*læticiæ et voluptatis*'. Douglas takes the lines in the same sense in his *Eneados* and his epigraph for this section (c. iiii) seems to echo *LGW*. [2] *Sir Orfeo*, 102.

and which Gower's Medea reveals in her address to Jason after *their* secret 'marriage':

> Mi trust, mi lust, mi lif, min hele.
>
> (*CA*, v. 3643)

Chaucer's Dido is a hapless innocent trusting Aeneas's oath and 'goodly outside' (262–5). But Virgil mentions no oath: Chaucer infers it from the use of *connubium*, which he would take as involving the plighting of troth (hence he sees Aeneas as later failing to keep troth: 297) just as Medea's secret union with Jason in Gower (and in Guido) would be regarded as binding by the medieval reader.[1] Whatever Chaucer meant by 'al that wedding longeth to' he would feel in these cases the aptness of Ovid's *Fungitur in vobis munere legis amor*—'love serves the function of law' (*Ars Amatoria*, ii. 158). And indeed he is reading Virgil, as Ovid himself had taught him to do, through Ovid's eyes. This 'humble trewe wyf' who is forsaken by a plausible traveller is not so much the queen of Carthage as the heroine for whom Ovid composed the pathetic epistle in *Heroides*, vii; and that Chaucer had this letter in mind becomes clear when he later regrets that it

---

[1] The *connubium* of Dido and Aeneas in *Aen.* iv probably prompted the scene of Jason and Medea's espousals in Guido and hence in *Jason et Medée* and in Gower (*CA*, v. 3482 ff.), as in Boccaccio's *Filocolo*, ii. 165–83, which has been considered to be the original of the scene of the secret meeting of Troilus and Criseyde in Chaucer (*Tr.* iii. 519–1190). Chaucer, however, is sparing of the terms which might imply that this last was equivalent to a secret marriage: the interchange of rings takes place playfully (iii. 1368), *after* the consummation; yet Hymen is one of the gods Troilus invokes (1288), and he addresses Criseyde as 'wommanliche wyf' (1296) (whereas Gower's Jason in a similar situation calls Medea 'mai' (*CA*, v. 3662). It might be argued that Troilus did regard the union as a form of wedlock, but there is no evidence that Chaucer did.

Henry James constructs a similar situation in a very different social context, but makes the woman the betrayer of troth (in *Georgina's Reasons*).

'were to long to endite' (381). It would indeed have
checked the pace and upset the proportions of his poem;
but there is the ulterior reason that he had already 'endited'
it in the *Legend*. In the complaint that serves as its equivalent here only the conclusion approaches Ovid's manner:

> '"Lo, right as she hath doon, now she
> Wol do eftsones hardely,"
> Thus seyth the peple prevely'.   (358–60)

For if, on the one hand, Chaucer does not envisage a Dido
launching into the elaborate lamentations she gives vent
to in Virgil, on the other hand his taste would not admit
the conceits and epigrams which destroy any sense that
Ovid's Dido is heartbroken (*facta fugis, facienda petis* . . .
'you forsake what's done to seek what's yet to do' and so
forth). Not to overload Dido's plaint, Chaucer prefaces
it with a rhetorical excursus of his own devising: a means
of obliquely denigrating 'fals Eneas' by identifying him, as
does Bialacoil in the *Roman de la Rose*, with all 'shrewd
operators'; a means also of further varying the monotony
of pictorial narrative, for which in any case complaints
and preachments such as these are unsuited. Moreover,
this long *exclamatio* of the poet's (269–92), distracting our
notice from the pictures as it does, easily conditions us to
think of the following complaints and further *exempla*
(300 ff.) as ordinary poetic narrative, not as readings of
the murals; a point Chaucer quietly makes at the outset
by saying that he *dreamt* (313, i.e. imagined) that Dido
spoke and acted thus: 'none other auctor alegge I' (314).
It is he, and not Virgil or the designer of the temple, who
sees Dido wringing her hands (299); a characteristically
'gothic' gesture, originating in representations of Our
Lady at the foot of the Cross.

The long *complainte d'amour* which Dido utters (300–60), ancient as are its antecedents, is, like the *exclamatio*, a distinct medieval genre.[1] It can be found on the lips of a lover parted from his mistress (as in Henryson's *Orpheus and Eurydice*) or betrayed by her (as in the conclusion of Boccaccio's *Il Filostrato*). But far more often it comes from a woman in Dido's plight. No passages in Virgil were more familiar than those that had moved the young Augustine to tears (*Aeneid*, iv. 305–30 and 416–36), and several variations on them occur in medieval Latin verse, notably in the *Carmina Burana*.[2] Though Chaucer's Criseyde is hardly in Dido's case when she repeats Dido's weylawey—

> 'Allas, of me, unto the worldes ende,
> Shal neyther ben ywriten or ysonge
> No good word, for thise bokes wol me shende,
> O, rolled shal I ben on many a tonge;
> Throughout the world my belle shal be ronge.'
> (*Tr.* v. 1058–62; cf. *Fame*, 330–48;
> and cf. *Tr.* v. 700 with *Fame*, 345)

[1] Among many classical precedents we may note Catullus, lxiv. 132–201 (where Ariadne as depicted on an embroidered coverlet laments Theseus's treachery), and Ovid, *Heroides, passim*.

[2] *Carmina Burana*, Nos. 98–100. (The Benediktbeuern manuscript includes miniatures of Dido bidding farewell to Aeneas and her suicide (f. 77ᵛ, repr. in Hilka and Schumann's edition of *Carmina Burana*, vol. i (1930), Tafel 2.) *Aen.* iv. 365 ff. was one of the *themata Vergiliana* used as early as the fifth or sixth century as the basis of rhetorical exercises (Comparetti, *Virgilio nel Medio Evo*, c. x *ad fin.*). An epistle of Dido to Aeneas is in *Anthologia Latina*, ed. Riese, 800–83.

For St. Augustine's response see *Conf.* i. xiii. 21 (*flebam Didonem extinctam* . . .). Bernardus Silvestris, on the other hand, read into the story the necessity for self-control, and this view found favour. As a text for passionate lovers *Aen.* iv retained its appeal till the time of *Manon Lescaut*, the hero of which says 'Je fis un commentaire amoureux sur le quatrième livre de l'Énéide... "Hélas", disois-je en le faisant, "c'étoit un cœur tel que le mien qu'il falloit à la fidèle Didon."'

—none the less her poignant phrases clearly echo Dido's. And by the same token the formal rhetoric in which Henryson clothes the Complaint of his Cresseid cannot disguise a similar debt.[1]

But neither Chaucer nor Henryson is mechanically playing an elaborate variation on a time-honoured theme. Chaucer is converting the convention into a vehicle that will imperceptibly draw to the forefront of our interest two major motives that lie adjacent to each other in *Aeneid*, iv, but which are not there linked. Virgil gives us in Dido the pains of passion; but for Virgil the conveyal to Jarbas (the rival suitor) of the news of her espousals by means of *Fama* is a quite separate piece of epic machinery chiefly designed to account for Jupiter's intervention later. It is Chaucer who, by showing the Carthaginian queen as instinctively aware of the reproaches that 'fame' will bring upon her hapless love, intertwines love and 'fame' in a fashion that will explain why Jove's eagle, in the next scene of the poem, can plausibly suggest to his captive-poet that tidings 'of loves folk, if they be glade' (644–5) are to be found in Fame's house.

All of Chaucer's sympathies, even while he shows her folly, are with Dido; all of Virgil's power goes to vindicate his hero. For the Roman poet the queen represents delights that must be put by; Aeneas still has to live laborious days: *Tantae molis erat Romanam condere gentem*. The Miltonic allusion comes in almost inevitably here for in Virgil this is the very point where Mercury presents Fame as 'the spur which the clear spirit doth raise'. The image is Ovid's (*immensum gloria calcar habet*) but it conveys perfectly the force of Mercury's

---

[1] Cf. *Testament of Cresseid*, 450–69, and *Fame*, 345–50. Henryson's substitution of fickle Fortune for 'wikke fame' bears out the suggestion made below (p. 147 f.). For Cresseid's final warning (561–72) cf. *Fame*, 269–85.

'Si te nulla movet tantarum gloria rerum
nec super ipse tua moliris laude laborem...'
(*Aen.* iv. 272-3)
If by the Fame of so sublime a Fate
He is not fir'd; and will no toil endure
For his own Glory ... (Trapp's rendering)

That Chaucer as well as the author of the *Roman d'Énéas*
should find no room for these two lines shows again how
preoccupied they both were with the hapless Dido.

Laus and *gloria*—in Old French they become *los* and
gloire—are the closest equivalents to *fame* in the modern
sense that Virgil or Latin literature as a whole provides;
and in fact 'clere laude' is the expression that Chaucer
will resort to when he wishes to distinguish the good or
modern sense of fame from the bad (1575-80). But to
Latin *fama* in any of the senses that it has for Virgil both
laus and *gloria* are antonyms—direct opposites. Virgil's
juxtaposing of *fama* (rumour) and *laus* (renown) within
a hundred lines (*Aen.* iv. 173-273) can hardly have
escaped Chaucer's notice; and it is such passages in Virgil
as this injunction of Mercury's that justify the later
characterization of Virgil as 'bearing up ... the *fame* of
pius Aeneas' (1484). Indeed, the distinction between
Fame and Rumour which is to be developed in the third
book may be said to be implicit in these hundred lines.

III

Dido begins her lament on a note of *astysmos*, or
restrained sarcasm: 'Is this how men behave—one new
mistress, or even three, every year?'—as if working it out
by numbers (301-10). This sardonic overture is not
integral to the complaint proper: for once Chaucer is

using his heroine as an instrument to expose selfishness
in love. It is the charge of 'newfangledness' brought elsewhere in his poetry against the false Arcite—and the
lecherous sparrow. Just as 'good fame' ('bonne fame' in
Gower's *Mirour*) will have its counterpart in rumour and
scandal, so the 'grete worthinesse' of love, taken for granted
in the Invocation, as in the third book of *Troilus*, is here
shown to be sometimes spurious. 'Goodly chere', 'frendly
manere' such as Aeneas displayed, may be all deceit. And
first of the motives for such falsity comes 'fame'—here
unambiguously in the sense of worldly fame, *kudos*, 'renommee' (this last being to be sure not unrelated to 'worship',
but far removed from the notion of inner worth of which
'worship' is but the outward reflection). It is a parasitic
kind of fame, this worldly glamour that attached to a man
said to be loved by a great lady or a great beauty. But as
a persistent if subconscious human motive it is real enough.

What love 'for frendship' (307) may be we know from
the *Troilus*; and there is something of Pandarus's cynicism
in Dido's subjoined 'seith he'—insinuating that such love
(which as between men Chaucer elsewhere celebrates
unreservedly) is not as pure and abstract as it professes to
be. 'Every wight', says Pandarus, when urging that no
scandal could arise from Troilus's liaison with Criseyde—

> Every wight, but he be fool of kynde,
> Wol deme it love of frendshipe in his minde.
>
> . . . . .
>
> Swych love of frendes regneth in al this toun,
> *And wrye yow in that mantel ever mo.*
> (*Tr.* ii. 370–9; no equivalent in *Il
> Filostrato* or the French version)

The third false motive Dido is still calm enough to scan:
'for delyt, Lo, or for singular profyt' (309–10). Again

Chaucer's other works provide sufficient gloss. 'Delight' is that of sheer physical gratification: so Chauntecleer serves Venus 'Moore for delyt than worlde to multiplye' (*CT*, B. 4535); whilst 'singular profyt', private and selfish advantage, stands in absolute antithesis to the virtues of a Griselda, concerned as she is only with the *common* profit (*CT*, E. 431); the cuckoo's self-identification with this virtue in the *Parliament* (507) is plainly ironical, since he really symbolizes those whom Sir David Lindsay was to characterize as

> Havand smal ee unto the common weel,
> But to thair singular profyt everilk deel.
> (*Dreme*, 909–10)

Gower's priest Genius specifically distinguishes this 'covetise' from love of a woman for her beauty, grace, or virtue:

> For in non other wise hem longeth
> To love, bot thei profit finde;
> (*CA*, v. 2526–7 ff.)

This subcategory of the selfish, added almost as an after-thought, provides a stinging tail for the exordium, and by her interjected 'Lo' Dido almost involuntarily identifies Aeneas with this special branch of falsity. It would be altogether beneath the dignity of the story to suggest that he was actuated by lust. But that he had reaped material gain (viz. the refitting of his ships) from his meeting with Dido there could be no question.

Yet the reproach implicit in this final phrase gives way to a moving plea for pity: 'Allas, my swete herte . . . slee me not! go not away!' (315–17). Here it is Dido herself, not the poet of l. 258, who reveals that Aeneas is her very life—to part from him is death (323); and her appeal to

'your bonde That ye han sworn with your right honde' is
the more powerful because Chaucer allows no place to
Aeneas's reply, with its flat denial of any plighted troth:

> nec conjugis umquam
> praetendi taedas aut haec in foedera veni.
>   (*Aen*. iv. 338–9)
> (For I pretendit nevir, be na meyn,
> With ȝou to mak the band of mariage . . .)

Thus Chaucer forces us to construe Aeneas's flight as the
perfidy that Dido in Virgil claims it is (*Aen*. iv. 421).
His struggle against love is ignored; and the force of the
pietas that requires him to obey divine command—thrice
emphasized by Virgil (*Aen*. iv. 331–2, 393–6, 440)—is
only once, and that belatedly, alluded to. The pattern of
swift turns and divagations in Dido's complaint has some
precedent in the *Aeneid*; but that Chaucer is working to
different ends from Virgil is evident from the reduction
that the notable *descriptio* of *Fama* undergoes: the twenty-
five lines of *Aeneid*, iv. 173–97 dwindle to two:

> O wikke fame! for ther nis
> Nothing so swift, lo, as she is;   (349–50)

and by being put into Dido's mouth they take on a
radically new value and reference. In Virgil *Fama, tam
ficti pravique tenax quam nuntia veri* (188: 'Als weil ramem-
bring fenȝeit and schrewit sawys As scho the treuth and
verite furth schawis'), spreads malicious rumour as soon
as it is known that the queen and Aeneas have been alone
together in the cave; and the rumour depicts them as *both*
loving for 'singular profit': this being exactly the implication of

> nunc hiemem inter se luxu, quam longa, fovere
> regnorum immemores turpique cupidine captos.   (193–4)

(—And how the wyntir seeson betwix thame tway
Thay spend in lang reffell, lust, and play,
Of thar realmys na thing remembering,
In fowle delyt ybond by Cupid king;)

an implication that can find no place in Chaucer's *schema*
since his Dido scorns such 'profit'. The *exclamatio* that
Chaucer gives her both abbreviates and generalizes
Virgil's opening couplet—

Extemplo Libyae magnas it Fama per urbes,
Fama, malum qua non aliud velocius ullum—

and glances at the same time at Virgil's later use of *impia
Fama*, in a rather different meaning from *wikke* and in
a very different context (the report of 'unscrupulous
Rumour' that the Trojan ships are about to sail, *Aen.* iv.
298; where Dido has in mind the turpitude that ignores
the decencies of human relationships). What else of
Virgil's description of *Fama* Chaucer found apposite to
his general as distinct from his immediate purpose will
appear in the analysis of Book III.[1]

To a Dido who is so distressed by slander and the lasting
loss of reputation Chaucer can decorously add a trait from
the Dido of Ovid's Epistles. 'That I have doon, rekever
I never' (354) is not so much a lament for the loss of
chastity as an expression of grief that

'I shal be seyd, allas
Yshamed be through Eneas'; (355–6)

---

[1] Virgil's figuring of Fame's delight when *haec . . . multiplici populos sermone
replebat* (189) and of her indifference to truth (*facta atque infacta canebat*: 190),
provides verbal suggestions for two lines in Book I. From the former line
comes Dido's surmise as to what 'seyth the peple prevely' (360), from the latter
Chaucer's own stark comment 'But that is doon, is not to done' (361). *Troilus
and Criseyde*, iv. 659–61 ('The swifte Fame . . . yfled with preste wings . . .'),
which appears to render *Aen.* iv. 173–5, in fact follows Boccaccio's version in
Il Filostrato, iv. 78. See further p. 131.

This recalls the words of Ovid's Dido, who uses *fama* in a way that would hook them in the poet's memory:

> Sed merita et famam corpusque animumque pudicum
> Cum mala perdiderim, perdere verba leve est.
>
> 　　　　　　　　　　　　　　(*Her.* vii. 5–6)

IV

And now Chaucer takes a sudden jump, overleaping almost all the action that in Virgil leads up to Dido's immolation. The brief mention of Aeneas's imminent departure (365) brings us at once to *Aeneid,* iv. 554–5. This reading of Virgil ignores everything but the fatal effects that falsehood and rumour have on misguided love: and a reference to Ovid provides a curt conclusion:

> But al the maner how she deyde
> And al the wordes that she seyde,
> Whoso to know it hath purpos,
> Reed Virgil in Eneydos
> Or the Epistle of Ovyde . . .　(375–9)

The direction to Ovid is worth following: for the stories of betrayal that Chaucer now lists by way of *exempla* are all to be found in the *Heroides*, and in much the same order. The assertion that of the harm 'that hath betid for swich untrouthe . . . men may *ofte* in bokes rede' (384–5) is like﹣ wise not made idly: almost all the stories that he cites are to be found again in Ovid's *Ars Amatoria*, where Jean de Meun had met them and hence inserted them in the *Roman* immediately after Dido's 'legende'. Indeed the first, the tale of Phillis, so closely resembles Dido's that an allusion to it was almost inevitable. Like Dido she is a queen who befriends a stranger (Demophöon) when like

Aeneas he is beset by storms after the fall of Troy. He becomes the love of his *hospita* (Ovid uses Virgil's term) who, again like Dido, offers him the rule of her kingdom. Phillis too is disgraced in her subjects' eyes by her guest's departure to conquer another kingdom, and she too turns to suicide, considering Dido's method before she finally decides to hang herself. Illustrators of the *Roman* often depicted the two events in the same miniature;[1] and perhaps Chaucer, as Kittredge thought, took his condensed account of her tragedy from the *Roman*:

> Phillis ausinc tant atendi
> Demophon, qu'ele se pendi,
> Pour le terme qu'i *trespassa*
> Don sairement e fei cassa.
> (*Rom*, 13211–14; cf. esp. *Fame*, 392)

In the *Roman* the tale of Dido and reflections thereon occupy thirty lines; in Chaucer, some two hundred. The remaining eight books of Virgil he disposes of in a seventh of this space. Terse summaries of the action of the epic lay to hand in several places[2] and it would be profitless to look for particular correspondences. Chaucer's interest, and his verse, temporarily sags (451–60) and the repeated copulatives are as tedious as those with which the Squire's Tale drags to a halt. For a picture of the underworld of *Aeneid*, vi, we are referred, almost brusquely, to Dante 'that hit telle can' (450). Thus even while preparing us to move out of Virgil's world into the Italian's he acknowledges that the first part of the *Commedia* is inimitable. The equation of *Aeneid* vi, with the *Inferno* is emphasized

---

[1] e.g. Douce MS. 371 f. 87ʳ, Pierpont Morgan MS. 132 f. 97ʳ, and some of the early printed editions.

[2] e.g. *Carmina Burana*, cit. p. 37, n. 2, above.

by the allusions to 'every tourment eke in helle'. The
pictorial sequence of Aeneas's fortunes is briefly, and
appropriately, rounded off with the scene in which

> . . . Jupiter took of him cure
> At the prayer of Venus. (464–5)

It is as if Chaucer had noted the echo in *Olli subridens
hominum rerumque repertor* (xii. 830) (this is Jupiter smiling
at Juno at the end of the poem) of *Olli subridens hominum
sator atque deorum* (i. 254) (which is Jupiter smiling at
Venus at the beginning, and reassuring her '*quando haec
te cura remordet*'). He thus contrives that the mural sequence
shall end with a picture of the Venus with whom the book
began. Yet the final pregnant prayer must be construed
as addressed not to the goddess of the Temple but to
Jupiter:

> The whiche I preye alway save us
> And us ay of our sorwes lighte! (466–7)

Once more associating poet and reader, as at the very
outset (cf. 'God turne *us* . . .', 1) he now moves into
a larger dimension, and away from the pagan scene. This
is the Jupiter elsewhere to be described as 'the king The
which is prince and cause of alle thing' (*CT*, A. 3035–6).
The god whom the pagans ignorantly worshipped he
knows, and now invokes, as the 'lord that madest us' (470),
the Allmover to whom he had prayed in the Invocation
(81–82). We are shortly to hear more of this deity's concern for men; and the god 'that made Adam' (970) will
be presented, like Jupiter, as author of the phenomena of
nature (966)—truly *hominum rerumque repertor*. Thus the
form of prayer here further prepares us for a change of
milieu. The renewed emphasis, as we leave the temple, on
its rich and ornate contrivance—

> Yet saw I never swich noblesse
> Of images, ne swich richesse
> (471–2; cf. 121–7)

—leads us again to think of that other temple of Venus with its pillars of jasper, painted walls, and bed of gold in the *Parliament*. And indeed there is at this point some likeness in the movement of the two poems. As in the *Parliament*, the dreamer now leaves the Temple; but instead of passing to Nature's grove, green and flower-bedecked, and resonant with bird-song, he finds himself in a flat and barren plain:

> Ne I no maner creature
> That is yformed by Nature
> Ne sawe;   (489–91)

It resembles that waste land of Morpheus

> Ther never yet grew corn ne gras
> Ne tre ne nothing that ought was,
> Beste ne man, ne nought elles.
> (*Book of the Duchess*, 157–9)[1]

It is specifically a *sandy* waste: denoting, like pale-faced Patience's hill of sand in the *Parliament* (243), and Spenser's palace of Lucifer (*Faerie Queene*, I. iv. 4–5), the decadent and the illusory. And—as if to recall the barren loves of Dido, whose worst regret in Virgil is that she is left childless:

> —si quis mihi parvulus aula
> luderet Aeneas, qui tamen ore referret,
> non equidem omnino capta et *deserta* viderer
> (*Aen.* iv. 328–30)

---

[1] A free rendering of *Met.* xi. 600–1:
> non fera, non pecudes, non moti flamine rami
> humanaeve sonum reddunt convicia linguae.

For the Chaucerian associations of barrenness cf. *PF*, 137 ('Ther he shal never fruyt ne leves bere') and the 'bareyne ile stonding in the see' on which Theseus left Ariadne (*CT*, B. 68).

If in my Court resembling but thy face,
Some young Aeneas plaid, I should not mourn
As one so quite deluded or forlorn

(Fanshaw)

—as if to hint at this last bitterness, Chaucer adds that the sand is

As smal as men may see yet lye
In the desert of *Libye*

—the desert that Aeneas was treading in solitary exile when Venus found him: *Ipse ignotus, egens, Libyae deserta peragro* (i. 338); the same *litus harenosum Libyae* where Mercury alighted with his summons to depart (*Aen.* iv. 257);[1] the 'wilsum land' that Dido had imagined in her nightmare:

semperque relinqui
sola sibi, semper longam incomitata videtur
ire viam et Tyrios deserta quaerere terra.

(iv. 466–8)

In Gower 'le desert q'est infinit' is a periphrasis for hell (*Mirour de l'Omme*, 1284).

V

It is the absence of any sign of natural life which leads the poet to think that he is having a bad dream of the kind he alludes to in his opening lines and here specifies as a *phantasma*, or illusion of evil spirits. Just so Gavin Douglas's dream of Venus in his *Palace of Honour* is disturbed by unnatural sights and sounds: a river

[1] Cf. Lucan, *Pharsalia*, ix. 382 ff.; the same book contains the account of the apotheosis of Pompey which lies behind the last scene of *Troilus and Criseyde* and which Dante twice refers to when touching on the transitoriness of earthly fame.

Like till Cocyte, the river infernall,
Impossibil that it had been a *river naturall*:

'no gairs no herbis war visibill'; 'the fisch elland *as elvis schoutit*'; the trees are 'combus, barrand, unblosmyt and unleifit', the soil 'nocht but mareis, slike and sand'. Chaucer's prayer to be delivered from phantasmata is made 'with devocioun' (494), which is to say, in all seriousness; models for it are in fact to be found in devotional manuals.[1] The heavenward glance at such a moment (495) would be a reflex action representing the instinctive shunning of the sterile and the sinister.

But with that glance he catches sight of a great live golden eagle, a sight excelling the golden images of Venus's temple even as Nature in the *Parliament* excels all the pictures in that temple. And as Nature in the *Parliament* can only be compared with the sun, so this royal eagle (itself figuring in the *Parliament* as first in Nature's hierarchy), hovering near the sun, seems to emit a sunlike radiance. The association with the sun belongs to that bestiary lore about the bird to which Chaucer alludes when he says that its 'sharpe look perceth the sonne' (*PF*, 331), and on which Dante, Spenser, and Milton, not to mention Servius, have occasion to draw.[2] Dante's reference

---

[1] e.g. the prayer 'keep [me] from illusions of evil spirits' in B.M. MS. Arundel 285, ed. Bennett, *Devotional Pieces in verse and prose* (S.T.S., 1949), p. 248. (Chaucer applies the epithet '*devout*' to himself—and to himself as a pilgrim: *CT*, A. 22.)

If ll. 480–91 are read as implying that the temple itself vanishes, a further element of 'faery' is involved: for similar phantom buildings see R. S. Loomis, *Wales and the Arthurian Legend* (Cardiff, 1956), pp. 139, 172.

[2] The passage in Servius is in his note to *Aen.* i. 394: cf. p. 32 above. Henry Vaughan's *Eagle* (*Poems*, ed. L. C. Martin, p. 627) resumes much of the traditional lore, and concludes:

> Nature made thee to express
> Our souls bold *Heights* in a material dress. [*n. ctd. on p. 50*]

to the bird's powers is especially pertinent, since it came into Chaucer's mind at this very point. When in the valley of Purgatory Dante drops into a profound slumber he dreams that he is borne up in an eagle's claws into the sphere of fire:

> In sogno mi parea veder sospesa
> un' aquila nel ciel con penne d'oro
> con l'ali aperte ad a calare intesa . . .
> Poi mi parea che, roteata un poco,
> terribil come fulgor discendesse,
> e me rapisse infino al foco.
>
> (*Purg.* ix. 19–21, 28–30)

That Chaucer had made this bird his own is evident from the proems of the next two books as well as from the action immediately following in the present one. But it has not hitherto been remarked that Chaucer fused this scene with one in a passage from the beginning of *Paradiso* which he had drawn on once already.[1] In that opening Canto the

The sun-piercing eagle early became the symbol of St. John the Gospeller. Thus in an Anglo-Frankish Gospel Book (Pierpont Morgan MS. 862 f. 144^v) the eagle hovers with a book above the saint, in a roundel inscribed: *Hinc aquilæ speciem celsa petentis habet: it quia verborum pennis super astra iohannes*; cf. Alcuin: '*Scribendo penetras cælum, tu, mente, Johannes*', cit. *Convivium*, 1963, p. 466. l. 2. E. Panofsky, *Studies in Iconology* (1939, 1962, p. 25) refers to a minia-ture of *c.* 1100 in which the eagle has acquired a halo resembling St. John's. Gavin Douglas, noting that the bird 'maid ministration' to Jove 'of the thunder and wapynnys the tyme of the batale betwix the god Dis and the Gyantis' says that the evangelist is 'verray Iovis egill and clepit son of thunder' (S.T.S. edition of *Eneados*, ii. 46 n.).

The eagle as a divine mentor appears in the dream-allegory 'Gregory's Garden' (*Medium Ævum*, xxxv (1966), 29–37). But it is unlikely that Chaucer knew this Latin poem, which perhaps belongs to the fifteenth century. The *Ovide moralisé* takes over the eagle's association with the saint and finds him prefigured in Ganymede: see Panofsky, op. cit., p. 214 and his text illustration (p. 171).

[1] See p. 7 above. That Chaucer studied *Purg.* ix closely is shown by his use of it at *Tr.* ii. 64, and cf. pp. 56–58 below. Indeed for him the canto proved to be one of the most 'fructuous' passages in all poetry.

poet beholds Beatrice, 'turned on her left side', and gazing
at the sun: 'Aquila sì non gli s'afisse unquanco' ('never
did eagle so fix itself thereon', 48). Following her gesture
Dante too turns towards the sun, and even while he gazes

> . . . di subito parve giorno a giorno
> essere aggiunto, come quei che puote
> avesse il ciel d'un altro sole adorno
> (*Par.* i. 61–63)

('suddenly it seemed to me that day was added to day, as
though he who is all powerful had adorned heaven with
another sun')—precisely the simile that Chaucer now introduces (505–6). And describing the flight of his dream-
eagle, he depicts his bird, like Dante's, as first wheeling, then
descending (cf. 'sospesa . . . a calare intesa'). There was
some excuse, perhaps, for Lydgate's claim that Chaucer
had rendered 'Dante in ynglissh'.[1]

In the *Paradiso* the image of the eagle-sighted Beatrice
serves to show that she can gaze unflinchingly on the
supernal glory. Chaucer's esemplastic imagination has
seized on the bestiary association suggested by this faculty,
and, having envisaged his glittering eagle as likewise
hovering near the sun, he substitutes it for the sunlike
Beatrice. The transmutation of diverse Dantean images,
the adapting of them to novel purposes, the swift dramatic
effect of the eagle's appearance—all these foreshadow the
developments, and the density, that make the next part
of the poem so rewarding, and indicate that the poet is
by now wholly absorbed in his creation. He would have
understood what Sir Walter Scott, a loving admirer,
meant when he wrote: 'I warm as I work.'

[1] Prologue to *Fall of Princes* (fol. 8*b*). Skeat took this to refer to *Fame*; and cf.
Englische Studien, iii (1900), 290, *pace* Toynbee: see Spurgeon, *Five hundred years
of Chaucer Criticism*, i. 38 n.

CHAPTER II

Speculum Naturale

or poetical physics

As an egle with his winges
Fleth above all that men finde,
So doth this science in his kinde.
                Confessio Amantis, vii. 630–2

The world did drop away
As countries from the feet
Of him' that leaneth in balloon
Upon an Ether Street.
                EMILY DICKINSON, on a
                balloon ascent at Springfield,
                                Mass., 1860.

I

THE interruption of the action at this point by a proem
to what Caxton calls the *liber secundus* prepares us for
a change of scene and atmosphere. The pause is deliberate,
and the position as well as the content of the proem counts
against the view that the poem as a whole is casual or
extemporized. The matter of this second book, as distinct
from the first, is to be an *avisioun* (513), one of those special
kinds of dreams distinguished at the outset of the work,
a kind which, in the light of the comparison with the
notable dreams of Isaiah, Nebuchadnezzar, and Scipio,
we can here safely take to cover dreams of divine origin.[1]
Yet this very comparison re-introduces that mock-serious,

---

[1] Eleanor's dream (516) being, if we take Tatlock's view (*MLN*, xxxvi,
95–97), an exception that proves the rule.

quizzical note that is heard in the first proem and is to be sounded again in the last. All three proems, in fact, are by way of providing light relief for the weightier themes to follow. But they are more than interludes: they contribute to a pervasive pattern in which the serious and unsolemn are interwoven; whilst this second preface has the im-mediate if incidental effect of preparing us for the semi-secularization of Dante's profundities.

The introductory invocation is this time threefold: to Venus, to the Muses, and to 'Thought'. The address to 'faire blisful Cipris' might be meant for Troilus's 'wel-willy planete' (*Tr.* iii. 1257), which Chaucer addresses in the same style in the *Parliament* (113) and which Dante too calls 'la bella Ciprigna' (*Par.* viii. 2). Robinson cites the beginning of the *Teseida*, where Boccaccio calls first upon the Castalian sisters, then on Mars, and last on

> ... tu, madre d'Amor, col tuo giocondo
> e lieto aspetto, e 'l tuo figliuol veloce;
> (*Tes.* i. 3)

But the very fact that these lines follow a prayer to the 'sorelle Castalie' indicates that Boccaccio's stanzas were still unknown to Chaucer, who can describe these Muses as dwelling on Parnassus 'By Elicon *the clere welle*' (522), whereas Boccaccio properly locates them 'nel *monte* Elicona ... dintorno al sacro gorgoneo fonte', and explains the allusions in his commentary, to boot.[1] Thus to invoke

---

[1] Both Chaucer and Boccaccio are perhaps independently adapting the triple reference—to Minerva, Apollo, and the Muses, made in *Par.* i. 8–9. Boccaccio's *Chiose* states that the Muses are 'tutte figliuole di Giove, e d'una che si chiamò Memoria, secondo che i poeti scrivon: Castalie le chiama per una fonte che è in Boezia, ch' ha nome Castalia, consecrata alle dette Muse. Elicona è un monte nel qual esse similimente dimorano'.

In the closing sonnet of the *Teseida*, Boccaccio again speaks of the *fonte Castalio*.

the Muses, either at the outset or at a turning-point in the action, was the prerogative of epic poets: Dante refers to them when he comes to the very threshold of Paradise, and Chaucer himself elsewhere introduces them to point the climax of his own poetic achievement and of Troilus's joy (*Tr.* iii. 1809–10). But here he is still half-mocking himself and keeping his readers on the *qui vive* as he quickly shifts from one stance to another.

Amongst Dante's allusions to the sisters of the sacred well he would be bound to notice the one in the canto of *Purgatorio* next to the canto (xxviii) from which he draws so liberally in the *Parliament*:

> O sacrosante Vergini ...
>
> .   .   .   .   .
>
> Or convien ch'Elicona per me versi,
> ed Urania m'aiuti col suo coro,
> forti cose a pensar mettere in versi.
>
> <div align="right">(<i>Purg.</i> xxix. 37–40)</div>

—a passage in which *versi* ('pour forth') would confirm his belief that Helicon was a spring;[1] whilst *mettere in versi* is precisely what he means by 'ryme' (520). And as Dante elsewhere (in his first reference, *Inf.* ii. 7–9) begins by addressing all the Muses and then specifies their mother Mente, Mnemosyne, or Memory,[2] so now Chaucer proceeds to address in particular 'Thought', which must here

---

[1] Dante may have misread *Aen.* vii. 641 (*Pandite nunc Helicona, deae*), Chaucer such expressions as *fons Heliconae* (*loc. gen.*): cf. Douglas, *Eneados*, i. 57. Deschamps's ballade to Chaucer (date uncertain) likewise speaks of 'the fountain of Helicon'.

[2] Cf. Boccaccio's commentary on the *Divina Commedia*: 'e possiamo dire, queste muse, cioè scienza, in noi già abituata per lo intelletto e per memoria, potersi dire figliuoli di Giove, cioè di Dio Padre e della Memoria (re)' (ed. of 1918, p. 199).

as in Shakespeare's sonnet, be interpreted as the power to
summon up remembrance of things past:

> O Thought, that wroot al that I mette
> And in the tresorie it shette
> Of my brayn . . .
> Nowe kythe thyn engyn and might!   (523–8)

This is an evident amalgam of Dante's

> O alto *ingegno*, or m'aiutate,
> O mente, che scrivesti ciò ch'io vidi
> qui si parrà la tua nobilitate
> > (*Inf.* ii. 7–9)

with the two variants of the same conception in the
Paradiso:

> (i) Veramente quant'io del regno santo
>   nella mia mente potei far *tesoro*,
>   sarà ora materia del mio canto. (i. 10–12)

(Only ten lines later Dante speaks of revealing the 'shadow'
of Paradise imprinted 'nel mio capo'—'on my brain'); and

> (ii) O diva Pegasea, ch gl'ingegni
>   fai gloriosi, e rendili longevi,
>
>   .   .   .   .   .
>
>   paia tua possa in questi versi brevi.
> > (xviii. 82–87)

('O Pegasæan goddess, who givest glory to genius, and
renderest it long life . . . let thy power be shown in these
short verses'); the first two lines of which would commend
themselves to Chaucer as giving Dante's view of the worth
of poetic fame.

In contrast to the twenty-five couplets of the slow-paced
prayer to Morpheus that prefaces the first book, this second
proem is crisp and quick, several run-on lines (512–13,

520-1, 525-6) producing an effect of eager expectancy. We are to look out for marvels—and editors ought not to anticipate them by inserting 'The Dream' as subtitle here. Chaucer himself makes it clear enough that we are still in the dream by reminding us of the golden eagle 'Of which I have yow told' (529). 'Having wheeled for a space', said Dante of his eagle (*Purg.* ix. 28–30), 'he came down, terrible as lightning, and snatched me up into the sphere of fire.' The bird that Chaucer had caught sight of now swoops in the same way, though Chaucer expands the spare phrasing of the Italian: 'Terribil come folgor' becomes

> But never was ther dinte of thonder
> Ne that thing that men calle foudre,
> That smoot somtyme a tour to poudre
> And in his swifte coming brende
> That so swythe gan descende;   (534–8)

Dante's simile of the lightning has led Chaucer to the image of the thunderbolt—*tunc terris subito fulminis instar adest*, 'and like a thunderbolt he falls', says Nequam of the eagle swooping on its prey; and the all-dreaded thunder-stone in its turn brings to mind an ancient instance. The 'dint' that killed the proud Capaneus is introduced again, less cryptically, in *Troilus* (v. 15). In both places Chaucer is drawing on his favourite Statius (*Theb.* x *ad fin.*—xi *ad init.*), and the 'tour' is that on which Capaneus was standing when Jove 'swift and terrible' hurled his bolt: *ille iacet lacerae complexus fragmina turris* (xi. 9); 'he lies grasping the fragments of the shattered tower'.

The bird that could carry Jove's bolts—no 'low or easie lift', remarks Henry Vaughan in his poem on the eagle—could easily bear off a mere mortal. Jove himself had taken on an eagle's form for the rape of Ganymede:

nulla tamen alite verti
dignatur, nisi quae posset sua fulmina ferre.
(*Met.* x. 157–8)

Even if Chaucer had not originally had this tale in mind,
Dante's allusion would have directed him to it. For Dante
saw himself in the same case and place as Ganymede
'quando fu ratto al sommo consistorio' (*Purg.* ix. 24). The
reference would not escape a poet who had been lately
conning his Virgil and who would recently have read of
Ganymede's rape in *Aeneid*, v:

quem praepes ab Ida
sublimem pedibus rapuit Iovis armiger uncis; (254–5)

Quham with a surs swiftly Jovis squyar
Caught in his clewis and bair up in the air—

so Douglas renders the lines, seeing in them the action of
a *raptor* or bird of prey, and hence appropriately using
'surs' (Chaucer's 'sours'), a term applied to a hawk rising
on the wing after seizing its quarry. The image from
falconry leads happily on to the simile of the next couplet:

Me caryinge in his clawes starke
As lightly as I were a larke   (545–6)

—suggesting not only the size and strength of the eagle,
the ease of its direct upward flight, but also the feelings of
terror in the heart of its victim.

The sensations of terror are recorded in Dante; but in
Dante they are the *effect* of waking startled from an all-too
vivid dream, whereas here they are the *cause* of a swoon:

. . . mi scoss'io sì come dalla faccia
mi fuggì il sonno, e diventai *ismorto*,
come fa l'uom che spaventato agghiaccia.
(*Purg.* ix. 40–42)

('I startled soon as sleep fled from my face, and grew pale just as a man does who freezes with fear.')

That Chaucer had pondered these lines is suggested by the eagle's rousing 'Awak', and is proved by the identity of his 'be not so agast' (557) and Dante's 'non aver tema', the words of comfort addressed to his companion by Virgil (*Purg.* ix. 46); words that led to his recovery:

> a guisa d'uom che in dubbio si raccerta
> e che muta in conforto sua paura
> poi che la verità gli è discoperta,   (64–66)

(as a man who in dread is reassured and changes his fear to comfort when the truth is revealed to him):

just so is Chaucer brought back to life by the eagle's 'goodly' address (563–7). It is 'goodly' precisely because it does this, and the contrast is with the rude awakening from pleasant dreams in ordinary life, not (*pace* the imaginative biographers) with the usual early morning mood of a shrewish spouse. The 'vois and stevene' (561) is a 'mannes vois', such as that of the servant summoned to his bedside in the *Book of the Duchess* (45–48). It is one of those domestic touches that assist in establishing the poet's *persona* as something more than a lay-figure. They form one of the distinctive enlargements Chaucer made to the Vision as a literary genre, and create the illusion that we 'see him plain'. Gavin Douglas, as shown by his self-presentation in the *Palace of Honour*, was one of the first to appreciate their effect.

Nothing better illustrates the Chaucerian amalgam of earnest and game than the little dialogue that now follows as the dreamer takes heart of grace. 'What a nuisance you are', says the eagle in mild banter, implying that his burden is no longer limp with fear, but moving his limbs. 'But don't worry. You stand to learn something from this experience [571-9]; it is for your *lore* and for your *prow* (profit). This last phrase could bear a variety of meanings, but *inter alia* it reminds us that Chaucer regularly presents himself as searching in and through his poetry for 'lore' as much as for 'luste', for 'sentence' as much as for 'solace'. At the moment, however, this assurance of the eagle's benevolence comforts his live cargo not a whit:

'O God', thoughte I, 'that madest kinde,
Shal I non other weyes dye?' (584-5)

—though there is a sort of desperate hope in his remem-brance here that the eagle (highest though he is in the order of 'foules of ravine') is only one of Nature's creatures, and obedient to that 'vicaire of the almighty lord', whose hierarchy of birds the *Parliament of Fowls* displays. 'Kinde' in that poem as in this includes not only animate nature but the universe that was created by the knitting of the elements, from stone to star. So the reference gains in point as the poet begins to wonder whether his lot is to be 'stellified'. To create another star or constellation would be to expand the universe, while to be transported to heaven without dying would involve a violation of the natural order. Doubtless we are to think of him as envisag-ing (in 585-9) these alternative possibilities as equally supernatural.

Which alternatives the precedents that come to his mind are meant to exemplify is not quite so clear. Certainly Enoch and Eli as were not stellified, but taken up into heaven. Chaucer has substituted the Old Testament figures for worthies cited by Dante in a different context—at the outset of his journey downwards into hell, when he begs Virgil to consider whether he is worthy to visit the nether world; Dante knows (from *Aen.* vi) that Virgil's hero had made the journey and (from the apocryphal *Visio Pauli*) that 'lo vas d' elezione', Paul the chosen apostle of the gentiles, had followed him. But why should *he* be allowed to go?

> Ma io, perchè venirvi? o chi 'l concede?
> Io non Enea, io non Paolo sono;
> (*Inf.* ii. 31–32)[1]

The English poet, frightened at the thought, not of a descent into hell, but of an assumption into heaven, parodies the pattern of Dante's lines, but enlarges them so that they become, when read in the light of his own confession that this was 'fantasy' (593), an engaging variation on the modesty-formula. Indeed, in Chaucer's hands the formula has become so integral to the poem that we barely recognize its textbook origin.

The balance between the pagan and Christian worlds represented by Dante's Aeneas and St. Paul, Chaucer keeps by adding to the biblical names those of Romulus and Ganymede. Romulus figures here (589) because of a story told by Livy, Ovid, and Plutarch.[2] Plutarch, to be sure, scouted it as contrary to Nature, but Chaucer found it in his well-thumbed Macrobius, for Macrobius had no such doubts; he thought Romulus assured of a place in the heavens (*caelum*) because of his practice of all the virtues, including courage (*In Somn. Scip.* ii. xvii. 8)— a reason that adds piquancy to Chaucer's disavowal of

---

[1] For Dante's knowledge of the *Visio Pauli*, see Theodore Silverstein, *Harvard Studies and Notes in Philology and Literature*, xix (1937), 231–47. Commentators who take Dante to be referring to St. Paul's entry into the third heaven (2 Cor. xi. 4) must explain the appearance of his name alongside Aeneas's as intended to point a contrast between two different kinds of otherworldly experience.

[2] Livy, i. 16; Ovid, *Fasti*, ii. 491–509; Plutarch, *Romulus*, 27.

any likeness in situation. It is barely possible that he took Macrobius's words to mean that Romulus was stellified; but neither Dante's nor Ovid's nor Virgil's narrative of the assumption of Ganymede suggests that the cupbearer became a star; and it seems doubtful whether Chaucer had in mind Bersuire's view (noted by Boccaccio, *De Gen. Deor.* vi. 4) that he was 'stellificatus' as Aquarius. When the eagle assures the poet that Jove has no intention of making him a star 'as yet' (a deliciously ambiguous reservation) he speaks in synecdoche: stellification being the first possibility that Chaucer had considered, assumption the second. The eagle's words do not require us to find examples of the former among the names cited.

Jove's bird (which, like Virgil in the *Commedia*, knew the poet's name without being told: see 558) is now presented as a mind-reader; and one remembers Scipio the African's remark to the same dreamer in a similar situation in the *Parliament*:

Hit stondeth writen in thy face
Thyn errour, though thow telle it noght to me
(*PF*, 155-6)

—reminiscent as that is of *Paradiso*, iv. 10, and of other passages where Virgil divines Dante's doubts and hesitations. Such percipience is appropriately attributed to the keen-sighted bird who had long been the accepted symbol of spiritual acuteness. But Virgil's gentle raillery never obscures his prime office as 'il mio conforto'; and it is after finding that the eagle has lifted him bodily to the ramparts of Purgatory that Dante thus describes him, and is assured that he need have no fear: 'set your mind at rest, we are at a good spot' (*Purg.* ix. 46-47). This incident in turn recalls—and perhaps recalled for Chaucer—the scene at the very outset of the *Commedia* when Virgil announces that 'to free thee from this fear I will tell thee why I came' (*Inf.* ii. 49).[1] Certainly the eagle's words of comfort seem to be a conflation of the two passages:

> I wol thee telle what I am
> And whider thou shalt, and why I cam
> To done this, so that thou take
> Good herte, and not for fere quake.   (601–4)

In the *Inferno* Virgil goes on to explain that he was sent by an emparadised Beatrice to succour Dante in his misery and reward his love (ii. 104 ff.). And such, *mutatis mutandis*, is to be the role of Chaucer's eagle, obedient to divine Jove as he is and cognizant of his purpose—yet with that trace of the paternal in his disposition which appears to characterize most guide/figures in the world of dream.

There is a certain pride and sense of status in the fashion of the eagle's explication. To reveal that 'I dwell with the god of thunder whom men call Jupiter' (608–9) is hardly the readiest way to put the poet at ease. But in retrospect it will seem delightfully typical of this garrulous and old/maidish bird. The configuration of the poem, moreover, requires that the image of *Jupiter tonans* with a far/flying messenger at command should be set in our minds before we come into the presence of the Lady Fame, who will likewise have her messengers and be able to command sound 'as loude as any thonder' (1681). For the present, however, the eagle's function is to reveal some of the marvels of Jupiter's creation; and to the degree that he does this the eagle outsoars pagan mythology and is touched

---

[1] Chaucer's close reading of this part of the *Inferno* evidently extended at least to Canto iii, which he adapts in *PF* (see Bennett, *The Parlement of Foules*, pp. 63–64).

by the Christian tradition that associates this bird with St.
John, revealer of the mysteries of the Logos and the
Apocalypse, and with other prophets, contemplatives,
and philosophers: 'illos vero suos esse gloriatur', says
Nequam, 'qui rerum arcana subtili penetrant intuitu' (*De
Naturis rerum*, I. c. xxiii). Hence two early commentators
on *Purgatorio*, ix, take both the eagle and St. Lucy to
represent the intellect and in particular mathematics and
astronomy—an association shortly to be made by Chaucer
also (see 974, 993).

But the Chaucer who had sensed the dramatic possibilities of a bird that could both speak and lift a living
human through the air would not overlook the more
mysterious eagle that appears in the *Paradiso*, and in the
very canto (xviii) on which he drew for his second proem.
At this point in his ascent through the spheres Dante is
passing from Mars to Jupiter; and in this planet's ambience
the spirits form themselves into the shape of an eagle,
apparently so familiar in Dante's day as Jupiter's proper
attribute that he did not need to identify it as such. Like
Chaucer's bird it is golden: 'si che Giove pareva argento
li, d' oro distinto' (*Par.* xviii. 96: 'so that Jove seemed
silver in that place, pricked out with gold'). And in the
next canto this eagle-shape addresses the poet, saying
'I' and 'my', just as Chaucer's eagle does:

> ch 'io vidi, ed anchio udii parlar lo rostro,
> e sonar nella voce ed 'io' e 'mio'.
>   (xix. 10–11)

(for I both saw and heard the beak discourse and utter in its
voice both *I* and *mine*.)

That the English-speaking bird will not be concerned with
the high argument and arcane mysteries of the *Paradiso* one
gathers at once from his colloquial affability, his everyday

phrases and similes: 'Seinte marie . . . parde . . . by my trothe . . . dombe as any ston . . . dar I ley . . . as a blind man sterte an hare . . .'. Nevertheless he does promise 'wonder thinges' as he conceives them—wonders that turn out to include not only strange tidings of love but physical phenomena and the mysteries of fame. It would be hazardous to suggest that in introducing the theme of tidings of love Chaucer was deliberately secularizing the Divine Love that Dante associates with the sphere of Jupiter, in which he sees

> lo sfavillar dell'amor che lì era
> segnare agli occhi mei nostra favella
> > (*Par.* xviii. 71–72)

(the sparkling of the love which was therein signalling to my eyes our speech);

forthere *amor* has none of the physical and terrestrial associations of Chaucer's poem. Yet it is worth notice that the association of Jupiter with Justice which is the basis of the canto in question is likewise made, if in more human, not to say humorous, terms, by Chaucer's bird when he represents Jupiter as a god who 'thorgh his merite' (669) apportions due reward in recompense for earthly 'labour and devocioun' (666).

The labour is the labour of verse-composition, the devotion is to Venus and to Cupid, here pointedly again called 'blinde' (617) and 'reccheles' (669) since he has ignored the poet's love-service.[1] This revelation of the narrator-dreamer as himself a hapless lover comes as a surprise—but then the poem is full of such surprises; and there is a gentle irony in this belated (though of course not

---

[1] Venus may be said belatedly to acknowledge the tribute of his 'songes and ditees' in *Confessio Amantis*, viii. 294 ff., where Gower perhaps deliberately alludes to this passage.

necessarily autobiographical) disclosure that the dreamer
too is one of those 'ilke lovers . . . that hopen overmuche or
dreden' (37–38), that he too would wish to 'stonden in
grace of his love' (85–86). We sense now that this is both
a wish' and a fear'fulfilment dream, reflecting both his
own absorption in the worship of love and also his role
as a poet concerned with the presentation of that worship—
he writes 'Of Love and of his servants *eke*' (625). The
attention given in the first book to the scenes of Venus and
Aeneas and Aeneas and Dido, and to Cupid and Venus
themselves, now takes on a new significance: the dreamer
was studying those figures, not like a visitor 'loitering with
a vacant eye' in a Roman gallery, but with the eye of
a poet whose constant occupation had been to praise
love's art, to find in all he saw or read 'mater of to write'.

All'judging Jove, says the eagle, has observed this
whole'hearted devotion; but he has also observed

> that thow hast no tidinges
> Of Loves folk, *if they be glade*.   (645)

The disclosure is unexpected, and momentarily disturbing,
since most previous references have implied a confidence
in love's felicity. It is as if there has risen to the surface of
the dreamer's consciousness an unease about the outcome of
such passionate love as had led to Dido's downfall and to
the sorrows of Phillis, Ariadne, and the rest. The hitherto
unasked question, we now see, was latent in the whole
Virgilian story as just presented; and the emphasis on love's
woes in the first book of *Fame* thus acquires a new interest.

Outside the dream frame of the poem Chaucer has
already (in ll. 81–89) spoken of the 'All'Mover' of
christianized Aristotelianism as taking cognizance of
lovers and as having the power to give them joy. The
identity of this deity with omnipotent Jupiter is implicit

in the eagle's discourse and is confirmed when he avers
that the poet lacks 'tidings' not only of love but of 'noght
elles that *God* made' (646). In the same fashion Criseyde,
without obnoxious anachronism, will invoke 'Jove,
auctor of Nature' in a stanza adapted from Boethius's *O
stellifer conditor orbis* (*Tr.* iii. 1016), while Troilus will be
given the verses *Quod mundus stabili fide* in the rendering

> So wolde God, that auctor is of Kinde,
> That with his bond, love, of his vertu liste
> To cerclen hertes alle, and faste binde . . .;
>
> (*Tr.* iii. 1765-7)

—a doctrine which Theseus, developing the same Boethian
text in his peroration, will urge as a reason for marriage:

> This firste moevere of the cause above,
> Whan he firste made the faire cheine of love,
> Greet was th'effect, and heigh was his entente;
> Wel wiste he why, and what therof he mente;
> For with that faire cheine of love he bond
> The fir, the eir, the water and the lond
> In certein boundes, that they may nat flee.
>
> (*CT*, A. 2987-93)

The fair chain of love, then, in this philosophy, binds not
only human hearts but the whole creation—'oght elles that
God made'. Hence in the *Parliament* the noble goddess
Nature, whose immediate concern is that those creatures
should mate whose hearts are *knit* together (626-9), appears
as vice-gerent of the Almighty Lord

> That hot, cold, hevy, light, moist and dreye
> Hath knit by even noumbre of acord.   (379-81)

Thus 'ne of noght elles that God made' does not represent
a mere afterthought on the eagle's part. Besides reminding
us that Jove, in Henryson's phrase, is 'of Nature God and

King', it points to an aspect of divine power which Chaucer rarely mentions without (as here, and in the proem to *Troilus*, Book iii) conjoining some allusion to the power of human love. As in Virgil Venus must in the last resort be ruled by Jupiter, so here Jupiter is not only cognizant of lovers' concerns but also competent to reward the well-disposed lovers in his own way—in effect, to give them a glimpse of a wider world. And as in the *Parlia-ment* Nature's plenitude, richness, and harmony are set over against the sighs and sultriness of Venus's temple, so here we are to move away from the discords and dis-simulations of love (685, 687) to a view of Kind—in the very act of compounding and composing the elements.

The eagle does not plainly promise that the dreamer shall be granted sight of these marvels. He speaks through-out of 'tidings', that is (primarily), of things to be heard; preparing us for the picture of the home of such 'newe thinges' (see 1886-7), which will always be presented as learned by word of mouth (2025, etc.)—though it is inter-esting that when Gower agreed to write 'some newe thing' for Richard II the result was the *Confessio Amantis*, compiled 'ex variis cronicis, historiis, poetarum philo-sophorumque dictis' (*CA, Prol.* 51* gloss). For forty lines the eagle runs on in terms mainly negative yet all consistent with the poet's previous confessions of ignorance (in the prologue) or limited experience in the 'faculte' or art of love (248). As Jove's emissary the bird speaks as though he has divined these limitations. They explain his passenger's hermitlike withdrawal from common life:

> And noght only fro fer contree
> That ther no tyding comth to thee,
> But of thy verray neyghebores
> That dwellen almost at thy dores

> Thou herest neither that ne this:
> For whan thy labour doon al is
> And hast ymaad thy rekeninges,
> In stede of reste and newe thinges
> Thou gost hom to thy hous anoon
> And also domb as any ston
> Thou sittest at another boke
> Til fully daswed is thy loke . . .   (647–58)

All this is consistent with the *persona* of a poet who elsewhere presents himself as poring over his *Somnium Scipionis*
till dark (*PF*, 87); as dull of wit (ibid. 162, cf. *Fame*, 621);
as pensive, abstracted, 'out of this world':

> He semeth elvish by his contenaunce
> For unto no wight dooth he daliaunce

says Harry Bailly, and improves on the eagle's final 'dig'—
'thyn abstinence is lyte' (660) by adding: 'he in the waast
is shape as wel as I' (*CT*, B. 1890). And in the *Legend
of Good Women* the poet admits the general impeachment:

> . . . though that I konne but lyte,
> On bokes for to rede I me delyte.
>   (*Prol.* G. 29–30)

The antithesis between bookish retirement and the delights
of Nature—whether these be embodied in the *locus amoenus*
of the *Parliament*, or figured as in the *Book of the Duchess*,
where the contrast is with the reading of Ovid by night
and the sounds of horns and hunting in the spring—this
juxtaposition remains constant till we come to the Prologue of the Tales. There the dazed or diffident bookworm
has become a boon-companion:

> So hadde I spoken with hem everichon
> That I was of hir felaweschipe anon.
>   (*CT*, A. 31–32)

But the change has come about precisely because of the 'disport' that the eagle vouchsafes to him (664). For the 'game' is to conclude with a presentation of prototypes of the very pilgrims who constitute the Canterbury fellowship.

The likeness to the sequence that begins in the *Parlia-ment* when the dreamer is *hente* by African as here he has been *hente* by the Eagle (543) is underlined by the phrasal identity between African's assurance that 'sumdel of thy labour wolde I quyte' (*PF*, 112) and the bird's

> Thus this god, thorgh his meryte,
> Wol with som maner thing thee quyte.   (669–70)

Jupiter, that is, can 'quyte folk hir hire' just as well as Love is said to do (*PF*, 9); and his rewards will recompense those whom 'reccheles' Cupid ignores. African in the *Parliament* lives up to his promise that 'I shal thee shewen mater of to write' by leading the poet into a park where love's bliss and bale is to be set forth. By the same token the eagle avouches that he is to learn lovers' 'sothsawes and lesinges', their 'Jolite' as well as their 'Jelosie' (which jealousy is cause, according to the *Parliament* (252), of all their sorrows). The assurance is duly, if fleetingly, fulfilled when he sets the poet down on the entrance to the house of Rumour where a 'lesyng and a sad sothsawe' struggle for mastery (2095). The promised disport and game turns out to be, in some degree, at the expense of lovers. In like manner the Theseus who proclaims the excellence of the 'faire cheyne of love' can mock the 'heigh folye' of lovers whom Cupid often rewards with wounds and death; and can see that 'the beste *game* of alle' is that the adored mistress may know no more 'of al this hote fare . . . than woot a cockow of an hare'. The rival loves of Palamon and Arcite prove, indeed, a perfect instance of

> loves casuelly
> That ben betid, no man wot why,
> But as a blind man stert an hare.   (679–81)

This chiming of two proverbial phrases is not fortuitous.
If in the event not all the vagaries of love now listed at
length (674–99) are illustrated, that is primarily because one
purpose of the catalogue is to put love in its place. In
more than a literal sense this is a bird's-eye view of its
arbitrariness and irrationality; and it is because to the eagle
these aspects of love seem most significant that he associates
them with the arbitrary and irrational power of 'fame'
(663). Even as he reels off the list of love's caprices they
become comical:

> Mo discords and mo Jelousies,
> Mo murmurs and mo novelryes,
> And mo dissimulaciouns
> And feyned reparaciouns,
> And mo berdes in two houres
> Withoute rasour or sisoures
> Ymad, than greynes be of sondes . . .   (685–9)

To narrate or count them would be like numbering all
the corn harvested since time began (698).

This abundance of example is of a very different kind
from Nature's plenitude but it does resemble a feature later
attributed to another 'femynyne creature'—the Fame who
presides over the abodes of Rumour and Renown and who

> Had also fele upstonding eres
> And tonges, as on bestes heres.   (1389–90)

These ears and tongues obviously typify the almost magical
power by which rumour and report are transmitted and
magnified. And it is in this sense of 'rumour' that the
dreamer clearly takes the eagle's use of the word 'fame'; as if

associating it with the powers of the 'wicked' (and
feminine) *Fama* against whom Dido had railed. His
scepticism about these powers (700–2) shows somewhat
curiously inasmuch as his mentor never specifically asks
for credence in the belief that Fame hears *instantly* all the
'wonder thinges' just detailed. But his forthright avowal
that it

> 'Were impossible, to my wit,
> Though that Fame had al the pyes
> In al a realme, and al the spyes
> How that yet she shulde here al this
> Or they aspye it—'

this gives the bird a glorious opportunity to explain how
every sound must needs reach Fame's palace. And he
takes it with both talons.

II

As deputy for omniscient Jove the eagle knows the
contents of the dreamer's books as well as those of his brain.
So he can begin his lecture on physics by directing him to
a volume he knows to be in his library (712); and he forthwith renders almost verbatim the opening lines in Ovid's
description of *Fama*:

> Orbe locus medio est inter terrasque fretumque,
> caelestesque plagas, triplicis confinia mundi;
> unde quod est usquam, quamvis regionibus absit,
> inspicitur, penetratque cavas vox omnis ad aures;
> Fama tenet, summaque domum sibi legit in arce . . .
>   (*Met.* xii. 39–43)
> Amid the world, betweene Aire, Earth and Seas,
> A place there is: the confines to all these,
> Where all that's done, though far remov'd, appeare:
> And every whisper penetrates the eare.

> The House of Fame: who in the highest towre
> Her lodging takes . . .[1]

The paragraph in Ovid flows on for another twenty lines (to be incorporated in *Fame* later), and in it, we shall see, lies the embryo of Chaucer's poem. He has pondered and enlarged on almost every word of the Latin and made what in Ovid is inessential rhetoric the foundation of his main structure. The whole of Ovid's description could be detached from its context in the *Metamorphoses* without the slightest loss to the central narrative; and Chaucer may well have first found it so detached in some schoolbook or florilegium such as the anthology in which he found Ovid's tale of Ceyx and Alcyone. Yet he evidently had access to a complete manuscript of the *Metamorphoses*; and the setting of the description would be likely to engage his interest. For the role of *Fama* in Ovid is to bring to Troy the report that the Greek fleet is approaching:

> Fecerat haec notum, Graias cum milite forti
> adventare rates . . .   (xii. 64–65)

That is, her role is to spread ill news, much as she does in *Aeneid*, iv (and in some youthful Latin verses of Milton).[2] Indeed it seems possible that Ovid filched his *Fama* from that very book of Virgil, justifying his *imitatio* by presenting her in passive rather than active posture. For whereas in Virgil she herself personifies the swift flight of Rumour, in Ovid it is the rumours themselves, false and true, that take on life, flying up to the house whose doors are never shut—as rumours will do at the very end of Chaucer's poem (1951–8). What Virgil's and Ovid's *figurae* have

---

[1] All translations of passages in the *Metamorphoses* are from Sandys (1632). The version in the *Ovide Moralisé* (ed. C. de Boer), xii, 1588–1631, is of interest,

[2] Cf. his elegy *In obitum Praesulis Eliensis*, 8 . . . *centilinguis Fama* (*proh semper mali Cladis vera nuntia*) and *In Quintum Novembris*, cit. p. 155 n. 1 below.

in common are, first, *vigiles oculi,* the all-seeing eyes of *Aen.*
iv. 182—a line that Ovid characteristically expands into

> [Fama] ipsa, quid in coelo rerum pelagoque geratur
> et tellure videt, totumque inquirit in orbem;
>
> (xii. 63–64)

and secondly the power to bring terror to great cities:
Magnas territat urbes, runs *Aen.* iv. 187; *consternati timores,*
says Ovid (*Met.* xii. 60), and follows it with the story of
the fleet that is to attack Troy. Any medieval student of the
Troy story would attend to this account as carefully as to
the Aeneid itself. For Chaucer the resemblance between
Virgil and Ovid at this point may well have acted like an
electric contact, sending off a spark that revealed the artistic
potentialities of a poem planned so as to juxtapose Virgil's
Fama and her operations (as evidenced in the story of hapless
Dido), and Ovid's *Fama,* with her far wider activities.

Of the geographical position of Fame's palace Chaucer
makes at first no more than Ovid does. It is

> Right even in middes of the weye
> Betwixen hevene, erthe, and see;   (714–15)

Ovid says it is *summa in arce*—on a high mountain top; and
in due course Chaucer will give it a similar location
(1116); but Ovid evidently conceives of it as approachable
from the ground—*in cacumine montis e terra surgentis,* says
one commentator—whereas Chaucer interprets *orbe medio,*
'the centre of the world', in a larger sense: for him the
palace is so far removed from earth that it is accessible by
eagle-flight only: thus resembling the location in Dante of
Purgatory proper, which is as high as the sphere of fire
(*Purg.* ix. 31).[1] And as the eagle is Dante's, it is hardly

---

[1] The mountain 'higher than any that I had ever seen' which Ulysses
glimpsed (*Inf.* xxvi. 133–5) may have been Purgatory (or 'heaven-daring'
Teneriffe?); but it was 'bruna per la distanza'—its summit presumably hidden.

surprising that the perspective the English poet gains by the flight will be not unlike Dante's.

The twin descriptions in Ovid and Virgil owe their impressiveness largely to rhetoric. They abound in splendid tropes. In Chaucer these are to take on a life and habitation of their own: his Fame will appear as a forthright and very feminine divinity, her house (and Rumour's) is to be made of easily recognizable materials.[1] And he now introduces a different kind of actuality, the scientific, thus again drawing towards Dante's orbit and away from the classical poets. For all its spiritual profundity, Dante's poem is minutely precise in its physical details; and the ascent of the mount of Purgatory—not to mention other stages of the journey—provides occasion for scientific as well as theological discourse; Virgil's explanation of the apparent motion of the sun (*Purg.* iv), Beatrice's of the spots on the moon (*Par.* ii) being notable examples. In this Dante reflects the interest in scientific speculation and experiment that twelfth-century Aristotelianism had engendered. Long before Leonardo an Englishman, Roger Bacon, had imagined flying machines that could lift a man, with an engine and artificial wings like a bird's. Of this device Chaucer had probably not heard or read. But he brings English poetry abreast of Dante's—and creates a genre of which Bridges's *Testament of Beauty* is the last example—inasmuch as he now makes out of scientific theory the very stuff of his verse.

And these next two hundred and fifty lines 'of propre skil' should not be dismissed as an irrelevant digression into the didactic. 'This newe science' (the word itself—used in the *Parliament*—is new in the fourteenth century, but already included the modern range of meaning)

[1] The only hint of these in Ovid is *tota est ex aere sonanti* (*Met.* xii. 46) and even there the reading is questionable.

evidently fascinated Chaucer. Witness his book on the Astrolabe, an admirable piece of *vulgarisation* which we ought not to dissociate severely from his poetry and which may reflect the study of astronomy in the Oxford of his day, much as his speculations elsewhere on predestination reflect the concerns of contemporary Oxford philosophy. Witness too his fondness for Macrobius, fount of so much 'scientific' theory. Witness finally, again, Theseus's peroration, patterned like the eagle's discourse though concerned with the larger themes of 'speces of thinges and progressiouns' (*CT*, A. 3013). 'Lo, thou mayst alday see', sayd the eagle (737), pointing to an analogy. 'This maystow understonde and seen at eye. Lo—,' says Theseus to introduce a similar analogy. 'Right so say I', continues the eagle. 'Thanne may I seyn', echoes Theseus. Both are speaking the language of the Schools.

But Theseus is enunciating general propositions, not teaching an ignorant pupil. The eagle does not go quite so far as to call Chaucer a 'lewed man' to his face, but that phrase (866) reinforces the earlier reference to his ignorance of 'oght that God made'. He has told him at the outset that the adventure 'is for thy lore and for thy prow'; and *lore* he proceeds to instil like a patient dominie. He addresses 'Geffrey' (728) as if he were *in statu pupillari*, much as Chaucer himself addresses his *Astrolabe* to 'little Lewis, my son'. Nowhere else in the canon does the poet's Christian name appear. Dante too is only once named by his baptismal name, and then it is just at the point where Beatrice assumes the pedagogic role (*Purg.* xxx. 55)— a role resumed in *Paradiso* in the intervals of Dante's ascent through the heavens. In the *Commedia*, too, though for Virgil the poet is *figlio*, for others he is *frate*—in the same sense that Chaucer is the eagle's 'leve brother' (816).

Beatrice's explanation of the spots on the moon (*Par.* ii. 49 ff.) is at first sight no more pertinent to the main conduct of Dante's poem than is Nature's long exposition of the properties of mirrors and glasses while confessing to Genius (*Rom*, 18153–298) or the account of alchemy in the same work (ibid. 16083–148): all are vernacular manifestations of the thirteenth-century passion for encyclo-paedic learning. The eagle's disquisition can be justified far more easily than these. Yet Dante's seemingly trivial question about the moon, 'che son li segni bui [dark marks] di questo corpo?' (*Par.* ii. 49–50), has its own rationale: Beatrice having already revealed herself as cognizant of divine purpose in the natural world, she may fitly be asked *quaestiones naturales*. That Chaucer had perused this first canto of the *Paradiso* we have already seen. It presents Dante in a case much like his own at this point —astonished that he can be passing so lightly through the atmosphere (*Par.* i. 99); and it presents Beatrice as (on one level) an expositor of a philosophy of mutual order that clearly chimes with Chaucer's thought as embodied in Theseus's closing speech above-mentioned. And when the eagle begins to explain the laws of sound by asserting that each thing has its 'kindly stede' (730) and is moved by a 'kindly enclyning' (734) when away from its *locus*, he is merely rephrasing the doctrine set forth by Beatrice:

> Nell' ordine ch' io dico sono accline
> tutte nature, per diverse sorti,
> più al principio loro e men vicine;
> onde si movone a diversi porti . . .
>
> (*Par.* i. 109–12)

(in the order of which I am speaking all kinds incline, by diverse lots, more near or less to their principle; wherefore they move to divers ports)

It is good Aristotelian theory, hallowed by St. Augustine; and of the examples of this instinctive movement ('con istinto', *Par.* i. 114) given by Augustine one is found in Dante and two are in Chaucer. Commonplaces, to be sure. And that Chaucer knew them to be so is evident from the eagle's appeal, a few lines later, to common knowledge:

> Lo, this sentence is knowen couthe
> Of every philosophres mouthe,
> As Aristotle and dan Platon
> And other clerkes many oon   (757–60)[1]

—where 'dan Platon' suggests that Chaucer knew or knew of Chalcidius's version of Plato's *Timaeus*, and where 'other clerkes' could cover the Platonists of Chartres, St. Thomas, Nequam, *et al.* Yet certain phrases suggest that Chaucer here had the *Paradiso* before him. When he says of fire, smoke, and sound that

[1] The doctrine that each kind of body or substance had its natural place and natural motion in regard to that place was certainly Aristotle's (*Physics.* viii. 3, 4). Plato postulated that bodies of like nature tended to come together, hence a stone fell to the earthy sphere at the centre of the universe and fire shot up to the sphere of fire; and the Chartrains and Adelard of Bath accepted this view: see A. C. Crombie, *Augustine to Galileo*, 2nd ed. 1961, i. 30, 75–76. Macrobius (*In Somn. Scip.* i. xxii. 9); St. Thomas (*Summa* i Q 69 art. i resp. obj. 3), Nequam (*De Naturis Rerum*, ii. xvi) all touch on the theory.

Dante speaks also of the movement of fire upwards towards the moon (where the sphere of fire began) and the force 'that draws the earth together' (*Par.* i. 115–17). The Epistle to Can Grande cites Aristotle as the authority (*Epp.* x. 25):

continens se habet ad contentum in naturali situ sicut formativum ad formabile, ut habetur in quarto Physicorum. Sed in naturali situ totius universi primum cœlum est omnia continens.

The passage in S. Augustine runs:

Corpus pondere suo nititur ad locum suum: pondus non ad ima tantum est, sed ad locum suum ignis sursum tendit, deorsum lapis. Ponderibus suis aguntur, loca sua petunt.

(The body by its own weight gravitates towards its own place. Weight goes not downward only, but to its own place. Fire tends upward, a stone down-ward. They are propelled by their own weights, they seek their own places. (*Conf.* xiii. 9; cf. *De Civ. Dei*, xi. 28.))

> Alwey they seke upward on highte;
> While eche of hem is at his large,   (744-5)

'at his large' represents the condition that Dante covers negatively by his example of a creature that is sometimes constrained or twisted—'torto' (*Par.* i. 135); Chaucer applies the word in exactly the same sense at l. 775. Again: 'Now that you are free from bodily impediments', concludes Beatrice, 'you rise up naturally' [i.e. man's soul rises up naturally to God];

> No dei più ammirar, se bene estimo,
> lo tuo salir, se non come d'un rivo
> se d' alto monte scende giuso ad imo.
>   (*Par.* i. 136-8)

(thou shouldst no more wonder, if I judge aright, at your ascent, than at a river dropping down from a high mountain to its base.)

The eagle ends the first stage of his exposition with the same example:

> every river to the see
> Enclyned is to go, by kinde.   (748-9)

But all this is mere prelude for the theory of sound; a theory that Dante never alludes to, whereas Chaucer sets it forth at length, since his whole presentation of the functioning of Fame's mansion depends upon it. 'Soun', begins the eagle—his 'herkne' (764) hints at a pause for breath—'Soun is noght but air ybroken' (765). The form of the definition seems to be the poet's own, though in substance it is almost identical with that introduced by Macrobius when considering the music of the spheres: 'Sound is produced only by percussion of air'—*numquam sonum fieri nisi ære percusso* (*In Somn. Scip.* II. iv. 2); and of Macrobius's three examples—a staff lashing the air, a lyre, and a pipe—

Chaucer takes two (773). Macrobius in turn was probably leaning on the pseudo-Aristotelian *De Audibilibus*, which Chaucer also may have had access to in some form: the notion of air being 'rent with violence' when a pipe is sharply blown (775-6), though not expressed in Macrobius, is applied in the pseudo-Aristotle to sound produced by different kinds of oboe, and by the harp.

The theory of sound waves, on which the eagle bases the next stage of his exposition, has a somewhat different history, and Chaucer's introduction of it here, no less than the terms in which he sets it forth, suggests that his scientific reading, if not deep, was wide. It appears in embryo in Galen but receives its classic shape in Vitruvius, the great architect of the Augustan age: 'Voice moves in an endless number of circular rounds like the innumerably increasing circular waves which appear when a stone is thrown into still water and which keep on spreading indefinitely from the centre' (*De Architectura*, v. iii. 6). This theory had been rephrased in the thirteenth century, first by Adelard of Bath and then by St. Thomas in his Commentary on the *De Anima*.[1] But neither Vitruvius nor Adelard refers to the unseen subaqueous impulses, which Chaucer evidently introduces as analogous to the invisible movement of sound waves:

> Althogh thou mowe hit not ysee
> Above, hit goth yet alway under . . .   (804-5)

The whole comparison is of the simple kind that school-masters rejoice in; but Shakespeare was to apply it unforgettably to an attribute of Fame itself:

[1] *Aristotle's 'De Anima' with the Commentary of St. Thomas Aquinas*, translated by Kenelm Foster and Sylvester Humphries (London, 1951), pp. 279-84; see ibid., p. 278 for William of Moerbeke's version of *De Anima*, II. viii. 445-6 ('. . . if the striking is rapid and violent, sound results').

Glory is like a circle in the water
Which never ceaseth to enlarge itself,
Till by broad spreading it disperse to naught.
(*I Henry VI*, i. ii. 133–5)

All this scientific preamble, lucid enough and by no means flat, and eased down by a variety of everyday phrases, is firmly hinged into place when the eagle repeats his reason why Fame's place is where he had said it was (844): midway between heaven and earth and sea. We hardly expect to find any scientific authority cited for this essentially literary location; but in fact it sorts perfectly with Aristotelian cosmology, which conceived of the terrestrial elements as the skins of an onion: water (cold and wet) enveloping the earth (cold and dry), air (hot and wet) enveloping water, and fire (hot and dry) the air. Sound, being but 'air ybroken', belongs to the 'skin' within fire; and Fame's house must therefore be at the extreme edge of the sphere of air (and well below the moon; says Nequam: *Vera species elementorum in terminis reperitur*). Hence Fame can later call upon the winds in the same domain. And the circumstance that Fame's house is sur- rounded by pipers and harpers (1200 ff.) will seem less bizarre when we recall these early illustrations of the move- ments of sound produced by their instruments.

The modulation into dialogue (853–87) comes just in time to prevent tedium, being introduced by a deliberately repetitious and pedagogic passage (854–64), artistically justified by the irony that it is the dreamer we know as a poet who is assumed to be grateful for a simple explana- tion free from 'figures of poetrye' (858). Indeed, we are just at the point of forgetting that his interlocutor is a bird— just as we sometimes forget the *genus* of the disputants in the *Parliament*—when a vivid phrase re-establishes his real

shape and character; his reasons, he boasts, are so 'pal‑
pable'—his analogies, that is, so easy to grasp—that one
'may shake hem by the biles' (868).

But now the lecture is over. The poet's doubts are
silenced, and they can 'speken al of game'—they can con‑
tinue the flight without being troubled by whys and
wherefores. The poem becomes a tour conducted by an
ineffable guide, as pleased with his own superior know‑
ledge as with the astonishment of his captive audience. At
first the emphasis is on the rich variety of the extensive
view, as if in contrast with the sterile Libyan desert that
they have just left. The poet can see mountains, forests,
rivers, seas, towns, 'great beasts' and 'great trees'—marvels
such as Mandeville might have reported from the East or
the Antipodes, and representing, indeed, travellers' lore
rather than a nice concern for scientific naturalism. As
they move away from the known world the whole globe
takes on a different aspect. Soon it 'no more semed than
a prikke' (907). We do not need to have explored medieval
literature beyond Dante or Boethius to be aware that this
phrase brings us to an ancient and common *topos*—the
view of the universe *sub specie caelesti*. But by way of
warning us that he is not, or at least not here, vying with
his 'auctoritees' Chaucer characteristically adds a rationaliz‑
ing alternative:

> Or *elles* was the aire so thikke
> That I ne mighte not discerne. (908–9)

Even though the eagle will shortly assure him that he is
twice as high up as the Roman in the *Somnium Scipionis*
imagined himself to be, Chaucer would not have us
suppose that he pretends to any such semi‑divine revelation
as that vouchsafed to Scipio, or to Dante. He will show

his familiarity with their experience, as recorded. But the mansion which is the object of his dream-journey being midway between earth and heaven, he will never suggest, or need to suggest, that he passed beyond that middle point. Neither here nor in the paraphrase of the *Somnium* which prefaces the *Parliament* does he in his own person express any of the *contemptum mundi* that Cicero's fragment motivates, nor does he anywhere even aspire to attaining Dante's vision beatific. He hovers between two worlds, celestial and terrestrial, just as at the beginning of the poem he hovers between jest and earnest, faith in dreams and scepticism—and just as in the Tales he hovers between the road to Canterbury and 'thilke parfit glorious pilgrimage That highte Jerusalem celestial'.

It in no way follows that the comparison of the world to a pinpoint is mere rhetoric. Later references (at 916 as well as at 985-7) show that he was well aware of the many antecedents of the *topos*, and expected his readers to be so. 'From here', says Scipio according to Cicero, 'the earth appeared so small that I was ashamed of our empire which appeared, so to speak, but a spot [*quasi punctum*] on its surface' (*Somnium Scipionis*, iii. 7). Macrobius's Commentary duly explains and expands: 'Astronomers have shown us' (and the author of the treatise on the Astrolabe would note the phrase) 'that the earth occupies the space of a point [*puncti*] in comparison with the size of the orbit in which the sun revolves' (*In Somn. Scip.* I. xvi. 10; cf. 11, where he defines *punctum* as that which is too small to be divided). The prestige of Macrobius, if nothing else, led a dozen later writers to take up the comparison or to adopt the motif of which it is part. Lucan's version of it in *Pharsalia*, ix (the apotheosis of Pompey) introduces the heavenly laughter that readers of Chaucer know from the

last scene of Troilus; for though Chaucer's immediate
model there is the scene of Arcita's death in *Il Filostrato*
the ultimate source is Lucan's

> Vidit quanta sub nocte jaceret
> Nostra dies, risitque sui ludibria trunci

—lines remembered by Dante as he describes the view of the
universe from the sphere of Saturn: 'vidi questo globo Tal
ch' io sorrisi del suo vil sembiante' (*Par.* xxii. 134–5; in
the light of which we can hardly interpret Troilus's
laughter as cynical). From this point of vantage, adds
Dante, the earth looks like an *aiuola* (a small circular
threshing-floor such as may still be seen in Southern
Spain)—Dante's translation of the Latin *area* that Boethius
uses in the same context (Book ii, pr. 7, l. 20).

'Seestow any town?', the eagle now inquires. Scipio, in
Cicero's book, had been able to see from the celestial
heights the city of Carthage—to the Roman, the stage of
military triumphs, to Chaucer the setting for Dido's
griefs; and in fact the eagle's question echoes Africanus's
'*Videsne illam urbem . . .?*' (*ostendebat autem Carthaginem*).
Africanus was quick to point the moral: 'If it seems to you
so small, as it really is, why not fix your attention on the
heavens and contemn what is mortal? Can you expect
any FAME from these men? [*Tu enim quam celebritatem
sermonis hominum aut quam expetendam gloriam consequi potes?*]
. . . Vast wastes surround the inhabited spots. From the
Antipodes one could expect no fame [presumably because
they were thought to be uninhabited] . . . Rome is not
known beyond the Caucasus or Ganges . . . Who will
ever hear your name in the other portions of the globe . . .
and how long will those who now praise us continue
to do so?' Hoccleve was to make the point more

epigrammatically: 'I gat Affrik . . . My name was al
that there I gat';[1] and Chaucer was to remember the rest
in that discourse of Theseus's which so often seems to be
the quintessence of his philosophy:

> The grete tounes se we wane and wende.
>
> .   .   .   .   .
>
> He mot be deed, the king as shal a page.
>
> (*CT*, A. 3025–30)

Thus to someone as well versed in the *Somnium* as the poet
who had apparently worn his copy to tatters (it is 'myn
olde booke totorn'; *PF*, 110–11) Dante's brief re-
enactment of this scene in the Christian setting of the
Paradiso would at once recall Cicero's doctrine and his
concern with the limitations and impermanence of Fame.
Macrobius had underlined it: the reason for emphasizing
the earth's minuteness was that worthy men might realize
that the quest for fame should be considered unimportant
(*In Somn. Scip.* II. x. 3). At this stage, then, we can
reasonably claim that a cluster of themes becomes visible:

(i) Carthage as the city of Dido and of Scipio, the
fated city of whose doom Chaucer had read at
the very beginning of the *Aeneid*:

> Hinc populum late regem belloque superbum
> Venturum excidio Libya; sic volvere Parcas. (i. 21–22)

(ii) Dido is destroyed by *Fama* and hapless love, Scipio
wins fame by destroying Carthage; but

(iii) the sorrow of the one and the glory of the other
seem as nothing when viewed against the vast
splendours of the universe.

---

[1] *The Regement of Princes*, ll. 1162–3; ed. F. J. Furnivall, E.E.T.S., E.S.,
72 (1897), p. 42.

So far as all these themes appear in the poem, it bears the impress of the *Somnium*, more particularly of such parts of it as are not represented in the *Parliament* (where the total absence of the theme of fame from the otherwise close paraphrase of Cicero is noteworthy); but Chaucer's purpose is not to think Cicero's or Macrobius's thoughts after them, still less is it to out-Dante Dante. Though he flies high enough to see the fixed stars far more brightly than on earth (1015), he never soars beyond the region of the moon, the planet lowest in the Ptolemaic system. All the phenomena that he beholds:

> Cloudes, mistes and tempestes,
> Snowes, hailes, reines and windes,
> And th'engendring in hir kindes—   (966–8)

must be located in the region of air and fire lying between the sphere of the moon and the terraqueous globe: the winds being 'engendered' by hot dry exhalations in the sphere of air, clouds, mists, and the rest by cold moist exhalations. If this smacks of the cyclopedia it is because Macrobius's Commentary is itself cyclopedic, and almost all the poetic works touched by it retain some tint of it— and owe to it some of their diffuseness. Traces are thus to be found equally in the *Roman de la Rose* and in Brunetto Latini's *Tesoretto*—where it is the aged Ptolemy who answers questions put by a wanderer from Olympus:

> E iol mis ia ragione
> Di que' quatro aulimenti
> e di lor fondamenti,
> e chomo son formati
> e insieme leghati. (2934–8)

But even whilst revealing awareness of this diffuse didactic tradition Chaucer's poem retains its inner coherence. It is fitting that we should learn of the home of the winds, for Fame is soon to be shown summoning them to her service; and it is necessary to know that her house lies in the sublunary region, as this will explain her mutability.

For the despiritualizing of the Ciceronian creed the eagle's characterization of 'this large place, this air' (926–7) sufficiently prepares us. He tells his passenger not to be afraid of what he is to see:

> For in this regioun, certein,
> Dwelleth many a citezein
> Of which that speketh dan Plato.
> These ben the eyrish bestes, lo! (929–32)

The identity of these aerial burghers has been disputed, but there is no disputing the materiality of their milieu. The *Galaxias* of Macrobius here becomes as firm and localized as its by-name Watling Street, and the allusion to Phaethon's gallop in his father's 'cart' sharpens the image. Soon we are reminded that the constellations themselves are but beasts and humans 'stellified'. In these habitable regions the eagle can invoke St. Julian l'hospitalier (1022) or St. Clare (1066) without any impropriety; and the sounds here to be heard are not, as in Cicero or Dante, those of the empyreal music of the spheres, but the noisy clamouring of earthly men (1071); speech itself is here to assume a palpable body (1076–8). If at this point we recall the tone of the Proem and Invocation we realize that it was part of a deliberate yet subtle preparative for this world of humanized natural phenomena, wonders such as we meet in dream; a world in which Dante's high purposes and allusions are half-humorously transposed into a different key, though never burlesqued.

But this is to anticipate a little. For the present one must note that the sense of a human 'thickening' being added to an other-worldly philosophy is slightly strengthened by the eagle's comparisons with Alexander and with Scipio. The legend of Alexander's flight had been known in England for centuries, and early caught the fancy of English artists, of whom at least one gave to the birds who bore up Alexander's basket-frame the attributes of eagles.[1] Dante must have known the legend, and the mere presence of a passenger-carrying eagle in Dante would suffice to quicken in Chaucer's memory the story of Alexander's panoramic vista, as described in French romance—and as illustrated in at least one gorgeous manuscript, MS. Bodleian 264 (f. 80ᵛ). In that text of the *Roman d'Alexandre* the emperor says, in effect: 'By your help I wish to mount into the sky, to see how the mountains look from above, the heavens, the planets, the zodiacal signs, how the four winds speed through the air, how the clouds carry the rain . . .' (ibid.). And he has his wish. The birds bear him up through clouds heavy with moisture, past the home of the winds, close to the sphere of fire; at which point the stages of his tour become barely distinguishable from those marked in a more famous and more influential work—the *Anticlaudianus* of Alanus, which Chaucer certainly assumed his readers would know, or know of (986). Here and now he names alongside the Greek conqueror the Roman Scipio (miscalled 'King'), whose conquest of Carthage might be compared with the subjugation of Asia. Scipio cannot be said, strictly speaking, to have seen even 'in dreme', '*helle* and erthe and paradys' (917-18); all that

---

[1] The kingly figure with two bird-supporters on the early-twelfth-century tympanum at Charney Bassett, described by D. Talbot Rice (*English Art 871-1100*, Oxford, 1952, p. 156) as 'David' is probably Alexander.

Scipio learnt of hell in his *somnium* he gathered from his ancestor's account of purgatorial pains as reported by Cicero in what Pepys called 'that excellent and most divine chapter'.[1] Chaucer's reference to hell bears the impress of Jean de Meun: turning to the *Roman de la Rose* for some of the dream-lore summarized at the very outset of *Fame*, he would note that Jean refers to Cicero's story when scouting the belief that a dreamer actually sees spiritual substances, and heaven itself:

> Si con fist Scipio jadis;
> e veit enfer e paradis . . .   (*Rom*, 18367–8)

For Cicero as for Boethius the human spirit is lifted up 'beyond the smoak and stir of this dim spot Which men call Earth' to show, in the words of the *Parliament*, that it is 'ful of torment and of harde grace', that one should not 'in the worlde delyte'.

That Chaucer's purpose is something different from Cicero's is suggested by the eagle's next injunctions: 'Now turn *upward* thy face (925) . . . Now cast *up* thyn eye' (935). Here he will see not only 'the eyrish bestes' but the galaxy. Both give the eagle ideal occasions for pedagogical display; and for introducing the story of Phaethon apropos the Milky Way there was unexceptionable precedent.

'We are to know', says Dante in the *Convivio* (II. xv),

> that concerning this milky way philosophers have held divers opinions. For the pythagoreans said that once upon a time the sun strayed in his course and passing through other positions not suited to his heat scorched the place along which he passed; and this appearance of scorching was left there; and I believe that they were moved thereto by the fable of Phaëton, which Ovid tells us in the second of the Metamorphoses. (tr. Wicksteed)

[1] Pepys, *Correspondence* (ed. J. R. Tanner, 1926), i. 38.

In fact, Ovid begins to tell it in his first book; and the
Ovidian flavour of Chaucer's conceit 'the sonnes sone,
the rede' (942) derives partly from the telescoping of *sole
satus Phaethon . . . erubuit* (*Met.* i. 751, 756).[1] But the speed
and compression of Chaucer's narrative are quite un-
Ovidian. One word ('algate', 943) does duty for a hundred
lines of Latin; one line ('Til bothe the eyr and erthe
brende', 954) for another ninety. No room for a mention
of the thunderbolt (alluded to already at 534) which
Ovid's *Jupiter tonans* casts at the luckless charioteer. But
it was hardly possible in the Middle Ages to draw on the
Metamorphoses without drawing a moral as well. The eagle
smugly supplies his own variant of the usual reading of
the fall of 'Phaëton with his singed and shining hair' as
a warning against presumption:

> Lo, is it not a greet mischaunce
> To lete a fole han governaunce
> Of thing that he can not demeine?   (957–9)

—as if to remind his passenger that he, the eagle, is
emissary of this same Jove and that the poet had better not
'lepe and launce' (947). It all contributes to the complex of
meanings latent in the deftly phrased concluding comment: 'So *feithfully* to me spak he' (963): 'confidently'?
'assuringly'? 'firmly'? To exclude any of these senses
would be to diminish the force of a line that expresses in
miniature the poet's witty vivacity.

As the eagle draws towards a still more distant aerial
region the dreamer perceives that they have now passed
beyond the home of the elements and the place where they
are 'knit'. The knitting, we know from the *Parliament*, is

---

[1] The story may be read in Trapp's rendering (printed in Tonson's *Poetical
Miscellanies*, vi. 1709) which Pope commended: *Corresp.* ed. Sherburn, i. 105.

done by the same 'vicaire of the almighty Lord' who joins together living creatures. The poet's response to this aspect of creation is constant throughout his work, and now again finds ecstatic expression:

> 'O God', quod I, *'that made Adam,*
> Moche is thy might and thy noblesse!'   (970–1)

—God's action in creating man being of a piece with all his other works and showing forth both his power and his precellent splendour. Both attributes inhered in the sinless Adam, made as he was *ad imaginem et similitudinem nostram*; which is why Chaucer, following St. Bernard, says of the Virgin who restored that image

> Thou *nobledes*t so forferth our nature
> That no desdeyn the Maker had of kinde
> His sone in blode and flesh to clothe and winde.
>   (*CT*, G. 40–42)

It is by this divine standard of excellence that all other splendours must ultimately be judged—including the 'nobley' of Fame (1416) and the 'noblesse' of the pillars in her house (1424).

This part of the poem thus becomes a pæan in praise of the celestial part of the universe, corresponding to the pæan to terrestrial nature in the *Parliament*. Eighteenth-century poetry was also to hymn the spacious firmament on high, but to Addison 'no *real* voice or sound' could be heard amidst the radiant orbs which he views as a distant observer, embodiment of dignified and deliberate Reason. Chaucer mingles with the cloudy creation as familiarly as with the fellowship of the Tabard.

When he now looks down (964) he sees nothing of the terrestrial ball, only the 'eyrish bestes' and the cohorts of the mists and rains. If 'Boece' comes into his mind at this point (972) it may be because in the *De Consolatione Philosophy*, after instancing the fable of Orpheus whose backward look was fatal, promises—so Chaucer's own rendering runs—'to fycchen fetheres in thy thought' (cf. 974) 'by which it may arisen in heighte . . . swifte fetheres that surmounten the heighte of the hevene. Whan the swifte thought hath clothed itself in the fetheres it dis/perseth the hateful erthes . . . seeth *the cloudes byhynde his bak* (cf. 977-8) . . . passeth the heighte of the region of the fyr . . . til that he areyseth hym into the houses that beren the sterres [*astriferas domos*] . . .'. Ultimately he will come in thought to the soul's true country; and at this height he will see that the triumph of earthly tyrants is fleeting for they are exiled from this fair abode.[1] This will not be Chaucer's inference or emphasis—if he would not ape Dante, still less would he mimic the revered Boethius— and the realm of Fame lies far below that of Boethius's 'lord of kinges' (*regum . . . dominus*). But its mere remoteness from earth will mean that winged Fame will share with 'feathered thought' a view of earthly laud and triumph different from that of ordinary human kind.

Henry Vaughan, well versed in Boethius, says of the eagle that it can reach 'where man can travel only in a thought'; and its penetrative power would be a further reason why Chaucer should associate the flight with 'fetheres of Philosophye'. A ninth/century commentator had glossed *pennae* in Philosophia's *sunt etenim pennae volucres mihi* as *subtilissimae intelligentiae*, echoing a phrase that St.

---

[1] *De Cons. Phil.* IV. pr. i, *ad fin.*, m. i. The *metrum* owes much (as Chaucer and others realized) to Macrobius, *In Somn. Scip.* I. xvii. 10-11. Martianus Capella adapts it (*De Nuptiis*, ii. 98).
The image of a country far beyond the stars inspired a famous poem of Vaughan's (who translated other parts of Boethius), and (perhaps) a famous gloss to *The Ancient Mariner*, Part IV.

Gregory applies to the eagle itself.[1] Dante had this same *metrum* in mind when in the person of Cacciaguida he said that Beatrice, beautiful embodiment of divine philosophy, clothed him with wings: 'all' alto volo ti vestì le piume' (*Par.* xv. 54; cf. xxv. 49–50); and Chaucer is still attending to Dante even though his purposes are so different. The line would help to crystallize in his mind the conception of a philosophical flight; and albeit that the immediate concern is with natural philosophy, he is shortly to arrive at Fame's palace, where his point of view becomes philosophical in a more general sense.

Boethius makes no distinction—or rather, alternates —between the winged thought of the dreamer and the dreamer himself (Philosophy says 'I shal shewe *the* the wey . . . unto thyn hous . . . and I shal fycchen fetheres in thy thought by whiche *it* may arisen . . .'). He leaves us in fact with much the same kind of doubt that Chaucer now confesses to: 'Tho gan I wexen in a were' (979). Is the eagle really carrying him, or is it just his thought taking wing? Verily his case is not unlike St. Paul's when he saw the *tertium caelum* and heard things not lawful to utter (2 Cor. xii. 2); and he forthwith cites the Apostle's com⁄ment, for lines 981–2 render exactly *sive in corpore nescio, sive extra corpus nescio, Deus scit*. But lest we should think for a moment that he is simulating the Apostle's rapture (the nature of which has always exercised biblical com⁄mentators)[2] he at once adds allusions to purely literary precedents—Martianus Capella (985) and Alanus (986).

---

[1] 'By the word "eagle" is expressed the very subtle understandings of the saints': *Moralia in Job*, xxxi, xlvii.

[2] For the controversy see the account in J. A. Mazzeo, *Structure and Thought in the Divine Comedy* (Ithaca, New York, 1958), c. iv, and C. G. Hardie's review of that work, *Medium Ævum*, xxix (1960), 202.

The former reference would be primarily to the astrological discourse in Book viii of 'Marcian's' *De Nuptiis Mercurii et Philologiae* (which includes an account of the *galaxeus lacteus*), but also present in Chaucer's mind would be the descrip-tion of the flight of Virtue and Mercury into the heavens as described in Book i—where it is *Fama* who calls the roll of the heavenly choir: *cunctos nominatim vocabit Fama praeconans.* The reference to Alanus's *Anticlaudianus* follows inevitably, since the heavenly journey in that poem is patently modelled on *De Nuptiis.* In fact, as already hinted, Chaucer has been proceeding parallel to Alanus for some time: for the lines on clouds, winds, and 'engendring' correspond closely to

Aeris excurso spacio, quo nubila celi
Nocte sua texunt tenebras, quo pendula nubes
In se cogit aquas, quo grandinis ingruit imber,
Quo venti certant, quo fulminis ira tumescit (etc.)
(*Anticlaudianus*, iv. 332–5)

But both Alanus and Martianus Capella were describing flights of fancy taken by allegorical or mythological figures; and of this fabulous element in their work Chaucer's pseudo-solemn asseveration that 'sooth was hir descrip-cioun' (987) is an ironic reminder. It fits neatly with the eagle's sharp recall to actuality. As elsewhere, the bird divines the drift of his passenger's thought. 'Lat be', says he, 'thy fantasye' (992). He would clearly like nothing better than to give lessons in astronomy at this point of vantage. It was a fashionable subject among contemporary Oxford *cognoscenti*; and the author of the *Astrolabe*, not to mention the *Equatorie of the Planetes*, might be expected to have a relish for it. His reason for cutting the cackle— 'I am now too old'—probably implies no more (assuming it is to be read as authentic personal statement) than a certain shortsightedness. Froissart—and Chaucer has more

affinities with Froissart than with any other French poet—
excuses himself in similar fashion when Jonece, having
offered a sample lesson in astronomy, avers that he could go
on talking in that strain for three whole days. In his dream
the French poet confesses to a preference for a spring walk:

> 'Dont, chiers compains, c'est mieuls mes hès
> A moi deduire et resjoïr,
> Que ce ne soit à vous oïr
> Parler de grant astronomie;
> Car, au voir dire, je n'ai mie
> L'art ne l'arest sus tel ouvrage . . .'
>
> (*Le Joli Buisson de Jonece*, 1721–6)

But the didactic bird is not to be thwarted utterly, and
launches (997 ff.) into an *occupatio* summarizing the lore
in Ovid's *Fasti* that would have enabled the poet to
identify such constellations as Lyra, Gemini, and the
Pleiades. Once again we are being treated to fine foolery.
In fact Chaucer would know their positions well enough
and is taking the occasion to parody the tireless Alanus,
who had let his rhetoric play round just such a catalogue
of stellified birds, beasts, and humans as the eagle's:

> Hic ardet Cancer, urit Leo, Virgo resultat.
> . . . . preradiat Taurus Geminique Latones.
>
> (*Anticlaudianus*, v. 32–36)

—in short all the signs of the Zodiac. And when Chaucer
protests that the stars now shine so bright that 'hit shulde
shenden al my sighte To loke on hem' (1015–17) he is
mimicking Alanus's Fronesis (Prudence), who must needs
lower her eyes on the threshold of Jove's court:

> Hanc celi speciem Fronesis delibat ocellus,
> Quam penetrare nequit visus notamque requirit
> Materiam tanteque stupet miracula lucis.
>
> (Ibid. 37–39)

The eagle's concessive 'That may wel be' (1017) carries
another hint of smug superiority, wholly in character:
he, after all, can gaze unblinking at the sun itself. His
mere presence, however, proclaims that we are not in
Alanus's neoplatonic regions of calm and serene air—for
to them neither man nor bird could gain access:

> Que nullos hominum gressus volucrumque volatus
> Noscit, ab incursu rerum strepituque viantum
> Funditus excipitur, nullo vexata tumultu.
>
> (Ibid. 48–50)

III

Reading any other poet we might well think that we
had by now reached the translunar regions and the silences
of the eternal heavens. But the eagle's announcement of
journey's end comes almost bathetically in the phrases of
a footsore earthly traveller: 'Seint Julyan, lo bon hostel'
(1022), and no less unexpected is the rumbling that now
meets the ear. We are returning for a space to the Virgilian
and Ovidian strata of the poem. It is in Ovid that the *via
lactea* leads to a regal dwelling (Jove's); and

> Dextra laevaque deorum
> atria nobilium valvis celebrantur apertis.
> plebs habitat diversa locis: a fronte potentes
> caelicolae, clarique suos posuere penates.
>
> (*Met.* i. 171–4)

> ... by this the Gods resort
> Vnto th'Almightie Thunderers high Court.
> With ever open doors, on either hand
> Of nobler Deities the Houses stand:
> The Vulgar dwell disperst: the Chiefe and Great
> In front of all, their shining Mansions seat.

The rumbling is likened to Jove's own thunder (1040) but also to the beating of the sea against the hollow rocks 'whan tempest doth the shippes swalwe' (1036)—like the tempest (in Virgil's first book) that wrecked the Trojan fleet (*Fame*, 209). But this is merely an enrichment of the simile used by Ovid to describe the noises in Fame's house:

> nulla quies intus nullaque silentia parte,
> nec tamen est clamor, sed parvae murmura vocis,
> qualia de pelagi, siquis procul audiat, undis
> esse solent . . .

> *(Met.* xii. 48 ff.)*

> No rest within, no silence, yet the noyse
> Not loud, but like the murmuring of a voice.
> Such as from farre by rowling billows sent;
> Or as Joves fainting Thunder almost spent . . .

Ovid, however, would never have risked obtaining his effect by Chaucer's question-and-answer technique, which here has somehow the effect of involving or 'engaging', so to speak, both speakers in the phenomenon.

The noise 'of fals and soth compouned' is common to both Virgil's and Ovid's *descriptio*. Ovid, indeed, fancied the image, for he uses it not only in Book xii (*mixtaque cum veris passim commenta*, 54) but also earlier:

> Fama loquax praecessit ad aures,
> Deianira, tuas, quae veris addere falsa
> gaudet, et e minimo sua per mendacia crescit.

> *(Met.* ix. 137–9)*

> Fames bablings Deianira's eares surprise
> (Who falsehood adds to truth and growes by lies).

Chaucer's 'Fame', then, appears at this point still to be essentially the classical *Fama*, *loquax* and *mendax*, indistinguishable from Rumour, and sharing her magnifying power. The hint of this power given by both Ovid and Virgil (*Aen.* iv. 189 and xi. 139) had been amplified by Alanus when showing *Fama* as leagued with the Vices bent on destroying Mansoul:

> Nuncia Fama volat et veris falsa maritans,
> In superos Furias, in celum regna silentum
> Conspirasse refert, Manes Herebique tirannum
> Tartareum reserasse Chaos, fratrique negare
> Regna, nec ulterius pacem concedere mundo;
> Monstraque mentitur, monstris maiora loquendo,
> Dum sceleri scelus accumulat Furiisque furorem
> Addit et Eumenides solito plus posse fatetur.
>
> (*Acl.* viii. 305–12)

(Rumour flies on her errand and mingling false with true says that the Furies have conspired against the gods, that infernal chaos has been released and peace is at an end. Her lies take monstrous shape and grow more monstrous as they are repeated, while she heaps crime on crime, adds fury to the Furies, and claims that the Fates have power to do even more than yet they did.)

But, as in the *Commedia*, and in the *Parliament*, the guided visitor is to come to no harm himself. 'Hit is nothing wil byten thee', says the eagle (1044) in the phrase that Pan-darus will use to encourage Troilus. The flight is over and they make a happy landing on a 'made' road—a 'strete' (1049), suggestive of human habitation and civilization. But the only clue the eagle gives to the nature of Fame's 'place' (1053) is hidden in his 'Tak thyn aventure or cas' (1052): 'aventure' (cf. 1982) and crass casualty (cf. 679) will turn out to be distinguishing features of these celestial mansions. 'One question before you leave me', says the poet, again using dialogue to develop his theme, 'Does that noise come from living men?' The eagle's answer is perhaps suggested by the animated figures of Ovid's 'turn':

> confusaque verba volutant;
> e quibus hi vacuas implent sermonibus aures,
> hi narrata ferunt alio . . .
>
> (Met. xii. 55–57)
> Lyes mixt with truths, in words that vary still.
> Of these, with newes unknowing eares some fill;
> Some carry tales . . .

But it goes much beyond this figure to the profounder truth that as a man speaketh so is he: in this region speech

> wexeth lyk the same wight
> Which that the word in erthe spak.   (1076–7)

If rumours can be envisaged as flying, then they can plausibly be given human shape, and if human shape, then one corresponding to their human source.[1] The attention paid to this phenomenon conditions us for the other 'wonder thinges' that are still to come. But on another level it symbolizes an aspect of the imaginative process as operating in the poet whose influence has pervaded this second book; for the shapes embodying human speech correspond to those shades in Dante that embody the mental state of men in life.

The dreamer has now arrived at much the same point that he reaches in the *Parliament* when African leads him into the wonderful park: having first taken him by the hand and then given him a gentle push, African disappears from that story. So for a time will the eagle. But his promise that 'here I wol abyden thee' (1086) is to be

---

[1] In *The Great Divorce* a modern Chaucerian critic, C. S. Lewis, has employed a similar correspondence between the 'shapes' of human souls and their mortal thoughts.

fulfilled. Even in his *au revoir* his slightly bossy, patronizing good nature peeps through:

> 'And god of hevene sende thee grace
> Some good to lernen in this place.'   (1087–8)

And this also whispers, however softly, the same faint doubt whether the dreamer is capable of profiting by such 'good', that colours African's parting words:

> 'And if thou *haddest* conning for t'endite
> I shal the shewen mater of to wryte.'
>   (*PF*, 167–8)

Each couplet suggests that we are approaching the heart of the work, that its 'sentence' is shortly to be revealed. In *Fame* the suggestion is confirmed by the Invocation which immediately follows—at the head of the third book—and which drives home the point that the purpose of the work is much more than to daze and dazzle us with novelties.

CHAPTER III

The Palace of Fame

For deeds doe die, however noblie done
And thoughts of men do as themselves decay:
But wise wordes taught in numbers for to runne,
Recorded by the Muses, live for ay,
Ne may with storming showers be washt away

. . . . . .

But Fame with golden wings aloft doth flie,
Above the reach of ruinous decay:
And with brave plumes doth beat the azure skie
Admir'd of baseborne men from farre away.

SPENSER, *The Ruines of Time*

Shall it be Troy or Rome
I fence against the foam
Or my own name, to stay
When I depart for aye ?

A. E. HOUSMAN

I

A s Virgil leaves Dante to approach the mount of Paradise
alone, so Chaucer's winged guide, who has played a like
interlocutory role, bids the poet farewell when they
approach Fame's palace. Dante feels that he is growing
pinions for the flight ('penne', *Purg.* xxvii. 123) as Virgil
speeds him on to a region no pagan like himself may enter.
Though Chaucer's goal is hardly paradise, his study of
Dante's devices and architectonic does not stop at the end
of *Purgatorio*. When he begins his 'little last book' by
invoking Apollo it is primarily because *Paradiso* opens

with the prayer that Apollo will bless the work and grant
its maker the laurel crown:

> O buono Apollo, all' ultimo lavoro
> fammi del tuo valor sì fatto vaso
> come dimandi a dar l'amato alloro.
>
> (*Par.* i. 13–15)

(O good Apollo for the last labour make me a vessel of thy
worth so fashioned as thou requirest for the grant of thy loved
laurel.)

And behind Chaucer's appropriation of this prayer lies
the fact that he is the first Englishman to share Dante's
sense of the worth of poetry and of the act of poetic
creation. It is in the light of the long-standing suspicion
or disregard of poetry as such—still prevalent in Boccaccio's
day, as evidenced by Books xv–xvi of his *De Genealogia
Deorum*—that we must view the reverence with which
Dante regards Virgil, and the devotion with which
Chaucer follows in Dante's steps. Alanus, when he
approached the divine presence and the divine theme, had
bidden Apollo retire:

> Celesti Muse terrenus cedet Apollo,
> Musa Iovi . . .
>
> (*Anticlaudianus*, v. 270–1)

But Dante had made of the pagan God a heavenly muse.
In so doing he not only baptized his own poetry: he
vindicated all true poets.

Unlike Chaucer, Dante does not specify that Apollo is
'god of science and of light' (1091), but it is evident that
he invokes him because his future theme is divine *luce*, and
human knowledge and skill are inadequate to the task—
'vidi cose che ridire Nè sa nè pùo qual di lassù discende'
('I have seen things which whoso descends from up there

neither can nor may retell', *Par.* i. 5–6). Chaucer's humble
prayer has the same sort of propriety, even though his
appeal is for a different kind of illumination: *scientia* is
a recognized attribute of the Muses.[1] By the *disclamatio*
which begs merely that his meaning ('sentence', 1100)
should be clear, that his verse should please despite its
imperfections, he seems deliberately to be distancing himself and his 'little book' from his great exemplar, as if to
emphasize that he would never presume to essay Dante's
task or to present himself as a 'vessel or wineskin of the
deity'. Yet the 'art poetical' here ostensibly eschewed
(1094) is in fact to be a prominent theme of the book
inasmuch as its greatest practitioners are to appear in
dignified array; and against the abasement of this Invocation must be set the reliance on this same poetic art that
will be affirmed near the poem's end ('I wil myselven al
hyt drynke . . . As fer forth as I kan myn art', 1880–2).

A difference of intention does not inhibit Chaucer from
quickly resuming his close perusal of the Italian: 'And if',
he adds—after asking that his verse be made 'somewhat
agreable':

> And if, divine vertu, thou
> Wilt helpe me to shewe now
> That in myn hede ymarked is   (1101–3)

—then he will humbly kiss Apollo's laurel tree. The
gesture (possibly imitated from Statius) is one he associates
with another 'litel bok' in the so-called envy-postscript to
Troilus (v. 1791–2), and it adds a modest colouring to this
adaptation of

> O divina virtù, se mi ti presti
> tanto che l'ombra del beato regno
> segnata nel mio capo io manifesti,

[1] Cf. Boccaccio, *De Gen. Deor.* XI. ii (113*a*).

Venir vedra' mi al tuo diletto legno,
e coronarmi allor di quelle foglie . . .
(*Par.* i. 22–26)

(O virtue divine, if thou so far lendest thyself to me that I may show forth the shadow of the blest realm imprinted on my mind, thou shalt see me come to thy favoured tree and crown me with those leaves . . .)

He even finds a place for a phrase from the preceding tercet (which he has otherwise passed over for the moment as too solemn and mysterious for his purposes): for 'Now entreth in my breste anoon' (1109) is word for word 'Entra nel petto mio' (ibid. 19). And the allusion to Marsyas that follows in Dante will find its due place in *Fame* some 120 lines later.

Dante speaks of 'l'ombra del beato regno' that he wishes to reveal; Chaucer hopes for power to describe the palace he has dreamed of. And so far from 'doing no diligence to shewe crafte' (1100) he now embarks on much the longest *descriptio* in any of his works, one which surpasses the ecphrasis of Venus's temple in Book One to the same degree that the figure of Fame soon to be described would tower above Venus's statue. First comes a detailed and measured account of the setting and approaches to Fame's abode, both of which it is impossible henceforth to dissociate from her palace proper. It is built on a piece of slippery rock; and Ovid's *summaque domum sibi legit in arce* (*Met.* xii. 43; a detail ignored in the partial transposition of his account of Fame's house, in Book Two, 713 ff.) is immediately particularized to yield the assertion 'hyer stant ther non in Spayne' (1117): English soldiers (at least the Black Prince's) and English pilgrims who had seen the Pyrenees or Montserrat would appreciate the comparison, and 'castles in Spain' already suggested the

airy fabrics of daydreams.[1] Inasmuch as the rock shines
like glass (though more brightly, 1125) it does resemble
Venus's temple 'ymad of glas' (120)—a material in
medieval eyes as precious as it was brittle—and it is a fit
foundation for Fame's glittering palace of beryl. But this
hill turns out to be even less substantial than glass: it
becomes on closer view 'a roche of yse and not of steel'
(1130)—as impermanent as a motte of steel would be
enduring. The emphatic negative is not a mere trope; it
underlines the double *significacio*. The symbolism of the
glass Chaucer would find in the *Roman de la Rose*, where
it is applied to Fortune—an association that will prove
pertinent. Hence Lydgate's apophthegm:

> Fortunes favours be mad, who loke wele,
> Of brotell glasse rather than of stele.
>
> (*Fall of Princes*, v. 588)

But by presenting the hill up which he climbs 'with alle
paine' (1118)—signifying that all approaches to Fame
involve strenuous effort—as entirely made of ice he could
draw on a still older symbolism, that employed in Seneca's

> Quicunque volet potens
> aulae culmine lubrico:
>
> (*Thyestes*, Chor. ii. 391-2)

—verses that were to come home to the bosoms of Renaissance poets as they stood on Fortune's hill aspiring to
court favour and that were to be rendered by Wyatt and
more memorably by Marvell:

---

[1] Curiously enough, in Albrecht's *Jüngere Titurel* (c. 1270) it is
Montserrat that is chosen to bear the temple of the Grail, as magnificent in its
way as Fame's temple, and like it lit by a great carbuncle. The proverbial
'chastiaus en Espaigne' are mentioned in *Le Roman de la Rose*, 2442 (= RR,
2573); see Langlois's note.

> Climb at court for me, that will
> Tottering favours pinnacle;

but that long before had supplied to Alanus a distinctive
characterizing epithet for *Fortuna*'s twin sister *Fama*:

> Iam *lubrica* Fama per orbem
> Nature clamabat opus;
> (*Anticlaudianus*, viii. 148–9)

The poet's reflection that the builder on such foundations
is a fool needs no enlargement. But the next picture—that
of the castle actually standing on this 'sliper top' (1162)—
operates more subtly, to confirm the earlier suggestion that
Fame shares some of the attributes of Fortune, while being
superior inasmuch as it is in *some* respects (for *some* men?)
immune to chance and change: some names engraved on
this icy base do not melt away since they are 'conserved
with the shade' (1160). This part of the ecphrasis derives
indubitably from the description of Fortune's house in
Nicole de Margival's (?) *La Panthère d'Amours*, another
dream-poem, in which the author is escorted by birds
to a forest where the mighty god of love bids him seek
Fortune, since he is afraid of Amor:

> Venismes droit a la maison
> De Fortune l'aventureuse,
> Moult est la maison perilleuse,
> Car elle siet toute sus glace,
> Qui dure quel temps que il face;
> Mais moult belle est d'une partie,
> Et noble et de tous biens garnie;
> De l'autre partie est si gaste
> Que nul n'i a ne pain ni paste
> Et est ruineuse et deserte, *etc.* (1961–70)[1]

[1] Cit. W. O. Sypherd, *Studies in Chaucer's House of Fame* (1907), p. 118.
The date (e.xivc?) and authorship of the poem are still uncertain.

In due course Chaucer will characterize as 'aventurous' the wicker house of Rumour that is adjacent to Fame's 'place' and 'founded to endure' only so long as 'it list to Aventure' (1982). But the French poet was himself drawing, as Chaucer would recognize, on Alanus's rendering of the theme; and inasmuch as the *Anticlaudianus* provides the same basic pattern of a heavenward journey that Chaucer has adopted, its description of Fortune's dwelling-place is equally pertinent, albeit far more florid and 'conceited':

> Rupis in abrupto suspensa minansque ruinam,
> Fortune domus in preceps descendit, et omnem
> Ventorum patitur rabiem celique procellas
> Sustinet, et raro Zephiri mansueta serenat
> Aura domum flatusque Nothi Boreeque rigorem
> Parcius abstergit lenis clemencia flatus.
> Pars in monte sedet, pars altera montis in imo
> Subsidet; et casum tanquam lapsura minatur.
> Fulgurat argento, gemmis splendescit et auro
> Resplendet pars una domus; pars altera vili
> Materie deiecta jacet. Pars ista superbit
> Culmine sublimi, pars illa fatiscit hiatu.
> Hic est Fortune sua *mansio*, si tamen usquam
> Res *manet* instabilis . . .   (*Acl.* viii. 1–14)

This antithesis, expressive as it is of Fortune's double aspect, auspicious and drooping, Jean de Meun, as we shall see, adopts merely to elaborate. For Chaucer (who has likewise developed the duplicity of Fortune in the *Book of the Duchess*) it supplies at present no more than suggestions which he combines to produce a somewhat different image. Instead of a mansion gaudy on one side, decrepit in the rear, he gives us first the grandiose temple of Fame with its self-contained life and action, then, though much later, the inferior house of Rumour composed of commonplace materials and thronged with commonplace people. In Alanus the rock (described at the end of his seventh book) on which the house is built is for ever beaten by waves that now reveal and now obscure its shape; the flowers and trees that grow on it thrive or wither unaccountably—Chance governs all (*Acl*. vii. 425). Chaucer takes one hint only, and that a general one, from Alanus's rather turgid and tedious antiphrasis: it concludes with the figure of a wave that now overwhelms men, now lets them gasp for air, but mostly washes away all traces of their presence:

> Absorbet nunc unda viros, nunc evomit; istos
> Fluctibus immergit, hos respirare parumper
> permittit, sed quamplures sic sorbet abissus
> quod revocare gradum superasque evadere in auras
> non licet et reditus vestigia nulla supersunt.
>
> (*Acl*. vii. 471–5)

The emphasis here on the transience of human felicity would recall more familiar examples of the theme of Contemptus Mundi. Of these the most celebrated and the most often translated was the *Cur mundus militat*; and in that poem the vanishing of worldly glory is expressed precisely as Chaucer now expresses it. One side of the slippery rock of ice he finds to be carved with the names of the famous, but

> of the lettres oon or two
> Was molte away of every name,
> So unfamous was wex hir fame;
> But men seyn 'What may ever laste?' (1144–7)

Here, by means of the sardonic oxymoron of 1146 (fame becoming unfamous), Chaucer has given new force to the image in the Latin poem:

> Plus fides literis scriptis in glacie
> quam mundi fragilis vanae fallaciae . . .

Why does this world contend
For glorious vanity?
Whose wealth so subject is
To mutability?
As earthly vessels fail
Through their fragility:
So standeth worldly force
Unsure and slippery.
Characters raised in ice
Think rather permanent
Then earthly vanities
Wasting incontinent . . .

—so sang Nicholas Ferrar's community at Little Gidding.
But since Chaucer's Fame, unlike Fortune, is not to be
always or even essentially inconstant, he pictures this
dissolution as wrought by the sun that shines on one side
only of her hill—a new application, amounting to a
reversal, of Alanus's contrast of *clarus* and *nubilus*. On the
shady side, where the castle itself stands, the names are as
fresh as if they had just been carved (1152–60). Thus
out of the commonplaces about worldly vanity grows the
conception of a fame that endures for at least some folk
'of olde tyme'—the very opposite development from that of
Cur mundus militat, in which all the named famous
(Caesar, Tully, Aristotle, etc.) become alike 'silly
vermins food'.

Neither the *Cur mundus militat* nor the *Anticlaudianus* nor
La Panthère d'Amours dwells specifically on Fame,[1] and the
only writer before Chaucer to devote a poem to the theme
was Petrarch. His presentation of Fame is curious, but in
some details squares perfectly with Chaucer's picture.

---

[1] Though Alanus briefly indicates that the virtuous man should not wholly
despise it: *Acl.* VII. 126.

These are to be found in the fifth of the *Trionfi*, the Triumph of Time, rather than in that ostensibly devoted to *Fama* (the fourth); and the prime action (such as it is) of this fifth triumph arises from the hostility of the sun to those men whose fame might outlive them. Petrarch's sun, that is, has a personal interest in the dissolution of their renown: for

> . . . gif the fame of mortall men by death dois more
> incress
> Which ought by death to quenshed be and quickly
> brought to less,
> Than of my glore and excellence must cum my fall and
> end,
> and suddenlie, for which I rage, sall all to ruine tend.[1]

As the sun speeds away on his winged chariot Time rushes after him. But the folk who are guarded by poets and historians are seen as free from the fear of Time, for, 'escaping from the common cage', they have mounted upward. Later in the same *Trionfo* the dreamer learns that

> un dubbio inverno, instabile sereno
> è vostra fama, e poca nebbia il rompe;
> è'l gran tempo a'gran nomi è gran veneno.   (109-11)
> (Your fame no otherwise dois byid
> Than dois a plesant changeing blenk shyne in the wintar
> tyd,
> Which sone a litill cludde obscuris and brekis and maketh
> dark,
> And to great names great times to be a great and venne-
> mous spark.)

Human glory melts away even as the sun melts the snow ('Vidi ogni nostri gloria, al sol di neve . . .'). The Triumph

---

[1] The translation is that in *The Triumphs of Petrarke* (*c.* 1587) by William Fowler: see his *Works* (ed. W. H. Meikle), Scottish Text Society, N.S. 6 (1914), p. 118, ll. 15-18.

of Fame also includes the figure of eroding time: Aescu-
lapius and Apollo (the doctor not the musician) are so
closely shrouded that they can hardly be discerned: 'Sì
par che i nomi il tempo limi e copra' ('their names hidden
by time and worn away', iii. 69). None of these passages
would in themselves require us to conclude that Chaucer
knew the *Trionfi*. But if we accept Brusendorff's claim (and
it is wholly plausible) that the Clerk of Oxford's apostrophe to the 'stormy people, unsad and evere untrewe'
(*CT*, E. 995) depends on ll. 133–4 of the fifth *Trionfo*
we can regard it as probable that Chaucer had read his
Petrarch before writing *Fame* and before giving Fame the
same queenly role that Petrarch assigns to her. In the
sixteenth century Ariosto was to elaborate Petrarch's
allegory. Astolfo, on his wonderful visit to the moon
(*Orlando Furioso*, canto 35) sees names engraved on gold
tossed into the river of oblivion, whence some are snatched
up by crows and vultures (flatterers), and a few by a pair
of white swans, symbols of the poets who preserve the
memory of great men. Only the swans keep hold of the
tablets they seize, and they bear them to the temple of
immortality. And after Ariosto Spenser was to apply
Chaucer's own image of Fame's transitoriness to Chaucer
himself: though he was worthy to be filed on her eternal
beadroll, wicked Time, which 'workes of noblest wits to
nought out weare[s]' has quite defaced the 'famous moni-
ment of his verse' (*Faerie Queene*, IV. ii. 32–33).

　　Behind all these moralizings lies a long philosophical
tradition; and Chaucer's symbol of the transience of many
reputations, capped as it is by that question: 'What may
ever laste?', suggests that he was here remembering, *inter alia*,
that tradition's chief source in Boethius. It was Boethius
(enlarging on Macrobius) who had associated the bird's-eye

view of this little earth—the view seen during the eagle's ascent (905)—with the theme of the narrowness of human fame: 'Seestow nat', says Philosophy to him, in Chaucer's rendering of the *Consolatio* (Book II, pr. 7):

how streit and how compressed is thilke glorie that ye travailen aboute to shewe and to multiplye? May thanne the glorie of a singuler Romayne strecchen thider, as the fame of the name of Rome may nat climben ne passen? . . . thilke thinge that som men jugen worthy of preysinge, other folk jugen that it is worthy of torment . . . How many a man . . . hath the wrecched nedy foryetinge of wryteres put out of minde . . . Ye men *semen* to geten yow a perdurabletee, whan ye thenken that, in tyme cominge, your fame schal lasten . . .

In contrast and conclusion she pictures the soul in heaven where it 'rekketh of no glorie of renoun of this world'. She shows that fame as generally understood rests on *populares auras* (Cicero's phrase for the shifting breeze of popular applause), *inanes rumores, alienos sermunculos* ('other people's prattle'). It is this analysis that leads up to the development of the *ubi sunt* motif: '*Ubi nunc fidelis ossa Fabricii manent?*' 'What', as Chaucer puts it, 'is now Brutus or stierne Catoun? The thinne fame, yit lastinge, of hir ydel names, is marked with a fewe lettres' [*Si quot superstes fama tenuis pauculis inane nomen literis*]. Chaucer is obviously visualizing Boethius's phrase when he depicts names with their letters partly melted away (1144–5). And the humanist Petrarch was so much under the influence of this Boethian view of Fame that even when celebrating her triumphs he passes almost unwittingly from his catalogue of the famous to the questions 'Wher now dois lurk Zoroasters? . . . Quhair is Mithridates . . . Whair is he now King Arthure that at table round did sitt? Wheare be these Augustis caesars . . .?' The chief difference between the Roman philosopher and the later poets lies in his scepticism about the trustworthiness of writers and the permanence of their works: 'the whiche writynges long and dirk elde doth awey, both hem and eek hir auctours'.

The similarity between such muster-rolls of the famous dead as the *ubi sunt* passages in Boethius and Petrarch provide, and the catalogue of great men who become the sport of Fortune's giddy wheel even in their lifetime (a typical example, of Boethian derivation, and familiar to Chaucer, is to be found in the *Anticlaudianus*)[1]—such similarity would have been sufficient in itself to knit the *topoi* of *Fama* and *Fortuna* firmly together. Unstable fortune, in fact, is the concern of Boethius in the *prosa* (ii. viii) that immediately follows the '*ubi sunt*' *metrum*; and Chaucer took up the theme in the most serious and most Boethian of his short works, the *Balade on Fortune*. But in *Fame*, true to the dominant tone and intention, he is transposing Boethius's sentiments, as he has transposed Dante's, into a lighter key. The image of the rock of ice, frozen solid on one side, slowly melting on the other, is left to do its own work on the imagination, while the narrator temporarily reverts to his role of a natural rather than a moral philosopher. He has already (1120 ff.) posed as a geologist closely examining the rock to see of what 'congeled matere' (a new, technical phrase) it was made, and deciding that it offered a poor foundation for a tall building. Now he turns to the castle and considers its materials like a lapidarist (1183-4) and its construction like an architectural surveyor from the Office of the King's Works; swearing in everyday

---

[1] *Anticlaudianus*, viii. 58 ff. Some *ubi sunt* passages are assembled by E. Gilson, *Les idées et les lettres* (Paris, 1955), pp. 1-38, others by I. Gollancz in the Appendix to his edition of *The Parlement of the Thre Ages* (London, 1915).

fashion by St. Giles or St. Thomas as if he were in Cheap-side and not in starry regions inspecting a palace measure-less to man. Incidentally he thus obviates any risk of our interpreting his toilsome climb up the rock as an allegory of his own search for poetic glory. At the same time the steep ascent re-establishes in our mind the Ovidian con-ception of Fame's mountain as midway between earth and sky (cf. p. 73) and so at a point still below the moon: we should expect that earthly rather than supernal values and activities will still be dominant.

To describe the palace on the summit of the rock would, we are told, pass the wit of man (1170). It certainly deserves a prominent place amongst those architectural fantasies of medieval poets to which a recent writer managed to devote forty-five pages—without once mentioning this example so germane to his purpose.[1] It is 'so wonderlich ywrought That hit astonieth *yit* my thought' (1173-4)—precisely the expression used in the *Parliament* to convey his awe of that god of Love who 'my feling Astonieth with his wonderful worching' (*PF*, 4-5). The astonishment is of a piece with the wonder voiced at the very outset of the poem (2 ff.); and the similarity of his amazement in the *Parliament* before the *craft* of love to that here expressed at the building's *craft* (1177) happens to give point to the juxtaposing of the noble temple of Love in Book One and this castle of Fame in Book Three—a balance that is the formal basis of the whole poem. 'Riche', 'queynt', and 'curious' were the characterizing epithets for Venus's temple; and an emphasis on the 'craft' and 'curiositee' persists throughout the vastly more detailed description reserved for the castle. To the gold images, rich pinnacles,

---

[1] Paul Frankl, *The Gothic: Literary Sources and Interpretations through Eight Centuries*, Princeton, 1960.

tabernacles, and 'portreytures' in the former correspond the pinnacles, 'imageries' and tabernacles, 'al with gold be-hewe' in the latter (1189–90; 1306). Both descriptions illustrate the medieval pleasure in visual splendour. But equally there is no mistaking the implied contrast be-tween this artificial elaboration, however exciting, in both buildings, and the art that Nature makes. It is clearly spelled out in the *Parliament*, where over against Venus's cunningly ornamented temple of brass and jasper stands on a hill of flowers the abode of Nature:

> Of branches were hir halles and hir bowres,
> Ywrought after hir craft and hir mesure;   (304–5)

—*measure*, the beloved *aurea mediocritas*, making sharp the contradistinction from the luxuriant excess of builded fanes. If this is not made explicit in *Fame* it is partly because a principle of economy operates throughout the whole of the canon and not only within the separate works, and partly because Chaucer could rely on a general awareness of his implication. Certainly any reader of Alanus would sense it, for it is the same antithesis that he draws between Natura and the *Fortuna* to whom *Fama* is affined:

> 'Actus Naturae virtutis fabrica nostrum
> Non deposcit opus: nostro non indiget actu
> Tam celebris factura Dei quam singula ditant
> Munera Naturae . . .'
> (*Acl*. viii. 77–80 etc.; *Fortuna loq.*)

In loading every inch of Fame's vast castle with gold and ornament and figures dead or living, Chaucer may well have felt the impulse to go one better than the architectural fantasists whom Frankl analyses; but the attention devoted to these details is always subordinate to his final purpose.

The more marvellous Fame's castle is, the more striking will be the contrast with the suburban, not to say plebeian, abode of Rumour, her Cinderella sister. Here so much is statuesque; in the cage of twigs is all the ceaseless going on of life.

But for the moment it is the antithesis of Craft and Kind that strikes us—and that would strike even more strongly a visitor supposedly fresh from beholding the marvellous operations of Nature in the elements. Even the small harpers who ape the great are said to resemble Craft counterfeiting Kind (1213). And just before Fame herself is discovered (and significantly described as outside Nature's ordinary creation: 1366), the last detail of rich workmanship is introduced with a deliberate throwaway gesture: 'I needn't of course tell you that every surface of the hall was plated half a foot thick of gold' (1342-6). The intention and effect are, *mutatis mutandis*, much the same as Milton's when he gave Pandemonium its roof of fretted gold.

Whereas Venus's temple (in the *Parliament of Fowls*, 230) has pillars of green jasper, the entire structure of Fame's house is of beryl (1184), a stone of the same colour but with the quality of magnifying that is especially appropriate to Fame:

> And made wel more than hit was
> To semen, every thing, ywis,
> As kinde thing of Fames is;　(1290-2)

It thus embodies that *multiplex sermo* by which in *Aeneid*, iv. 189, *Fama* magnifies Dido's fault—a detail Chaucer had withheld from his adaptation of Virgil's passage in Book One. This magnifying power (and this alone) is the feature common to Virgil's *Fama* (the 'wikke fame'

or malicious rumour of Dido's *exclamatio*: iv. 349) and to
the goddess of Renown whose house this proves to be. But,
despite the arguments of several critics, we need not regard
this new aspect of 'Fame'—its identification with Renown
rather than Rumour—as an afterthought, a sudden twist
given to the sentence of the poem as a result of a reading of
(say) Petrarch's *Trionfi*. That 'Fame' was fissile material
Chaucer must have seen from the variable uses of the word
itself in his own day; and his Dido's allegation that
a man 'wolde have fame In magnifying of his name'
(305–6) has already introduced the sense of reputation that
brings renown.

The nice art of the castle's ornament, not to mention its
hilltop setting, testifies at least as much to Chaucer's
acquaintance with contemporary French artistic fantasy
as to contact with the marvellous romances considered by
Frankl; there is something here of the sophistication that
belongs to Jean Pucelle's illustrations for the *Heures* of
Jean d'Évreux and to the Limbourg brothers' pictures
in the Duc de Berri's *Heures* almost a century later. The
'babewinnes' (1189), the varieties of minstrels with their
miscellaneous instruments (1217–40), might seem trans-
planted from the lively margins of such manuscripts; and
when Chaucer later represents writers of the past as bearing
up the Fame of men and nations on their shoulders
(1429 ff.) we call to mind the caryatid posture that some
of Pucelle's figures take up. The sophisticated combination
of the bizarre with the familiar objects of everyday life that
distinguishes Pucelle's art can be detected equally in
Chaucer's array of classical harpers and homely pipers,
Virgilian trumpet and Catalan clarion, common jugglers
and courtly tregetours (1201–60). The musicians inhabit
these pinnacles as comfortably as they pace the battlements

of a tapestry of the Nine Worthies or the upper margins of the Bodleian Alexander romance; whilst the easy use of terms of art (peces, corbets, compassinges (quatrefoils), imageries, tabernacles, babewinnes) bespeaks the connoisseur Clerk of Works of the connoisseur king who made Westminster a centre of artistic and architectural activity.

But the sheer subtlety and multiplicity of ornament, like the increased density of similes—the windows are as numerous 'as flakes falle in grete snowes' (1192), the gleemen's seats are 'mo then sterres ben in hevene' (1254), the gold is 'as fyn as ducat in Venyse' (1348)—all this indicates that Fame's castle is more extravagant than any tapestry or painting. Perhaps it most closely resembles those lost miniature palaces of crystal and gold that in Chaucer's time began to figure as table ornaments along with 'subtleties' made of sugar or 'pared out of paper.'[1] A tabernacle made 'en manière d'un chastel' for Louis of Aragon (*c.* 1360) had double crenellated walls, the first with two 'portes bateilleresses' and two 'tournelles de cristal', the second with four 'tournelles' (and an image of Our Lady); a silvergilt piece had pillars on which stood men 'dont l'un joue de la vièle, l'autre de la guiterne, et l'autre de la cornemuse' (cf. 1218).[2] That the fashion

---

[1] The phrase 'pared out of paper' occurs in *Sir Gawain and the Green Knight*, 802, where it expresses Gawain's wonder at the ornate architecture of the Knight's Castle, and in *Purity*, 1408, where it is applied to the elaborate dish-covers on Belshazzar's table. Chaucer's parson (*CT*, I. 440) criticizes such costly table-ornaments 'peynted and castelled with papir' along with 'to greet preciousnesse of vessel *and curiositee of minstralcie*'—a phrase strikingly reminiscent of the *descriptio* in *Fame*.

[2] See Joan Evans, *RES*, vi (1930) 409 and n. 1. Cf. the splendid fifteenth-century censer illustrated in Burckhardt, *The Civilisation of the Renaissance*, Phaidon edition, pl. 165.

affected even ecclesiastical art we know from William of
Wykeham's ornate crozier, that miracle of craftsmanship
still to be seen (by pressing a button) in New College
chapel at Oxford. Chaucer's 'babewinnes' inhabit some
of its niches.

'Babuineries', in fact, were becoming an indispensable
feature in any work pretending to richness, and when
Lydgate described the vaulting of Priam's palace as 'full
of babewinnes' (*Troy Book*, ii. 654) he was anticipating
representations of that palace like that shown on the Duke
of Alba's late-fifteenth-century Franco-Flemish tapestry.[1]
They enhance the 'curiosite' of Fame's palace—a feature
that Skelton rightly seized on when giving Fame a house
not only empaved and embossed with turquoise and
chrysolite as well as beryl but also

> so curiously, so craftely, so conningly wrowght
> That all the worlde, I trowe, and it were sought,
> Suche an other there coude no man fynde;
> (*Garland of Laurel*, 461-3)

lines that reflect Chaucer's rhetorical as well as his architectural embellishments: for it is at the same point that
Chaucer introduces his *praecisio*, or impossibility formula,
insisting

> That all the men that ben on lyve
> Ne han the cunning to descryve
> The beautee of that ilke place
> Ne coude casten no compace
> Swich another for to make . . .   (1167-71)

The immediate purpose is to figure forth Fame's compelling power and attractiveness just as the temple of

[1] Reproduced in Margaret R. Scherer, *The Legends of Troy in Art and Literature* (1963), pl. 87.

Venus has symbolized the irresistible fascination of love. It is this goodly outside that draws the throngs of sup-pliants for Fame's favour. Milton was to present the temptation of worldly glory in almost identical terms:

> The Imperial Palace, compass huge, and high
> The Structure, skill of noblest Architects,
> With gilded battlements, conspicuous far,
> Turrets and terrases, and glittering Spires
> .   .   . pillars and roofs
> Carv'd work, the hand of fam'd Artificers
> In Cedar, Marble, Ivory, or Gold.
> (*Paradise Regain'd*, iv. 50–60)

Yet the very richness of the palaces depicted by these poets guards us against unqualified acceptance of their beauty as a symbol of worth. And the 'babewinnes' are not merely ornamental: various as are the applications of the term elsewhere, its transparent derivation (O.F. *babuin*, 'baboon') would indicate to any courtly audience such as Chaucer's that these grotesque figures were fit setting for the small harpers that gape at the great ones 'and countrefete hem as an ape' (1212)—another significant simile, heavy in medieval use with all the sinister connotations of apelike arrogance. Here, as Apemantus would say,

> The strain of man's bred out
> Into baboon and monkey.

To Robert Holcot, the gifted fourteenth-century 'classic-izing' friar, the 'babewinn' carved as a support for an architectural feature is a symbol of pretence and self-importance.[1] Thus even the external decorament conveys

---

[1] '... omnino similes sunt babbewyno, depicto et sculpto, qui collo, humeris, et brachiis et facie prominens, totam fabricam cum onerosa fatigatione se *simulat* supportare': Comm. on Wisdom, lect. clxvi, cit. B. Smalley, *English Friars and Antiquity* (1960), 167, n. 3.

the suggestion that Fame like Venus has a double aspect, that it may involve the false and the factitious; a suggestion that is to be strengthened as its equivocal working is revealed.

In 'habitacles' of the outer walls, cheek by jowl with the 'babewinnes' and other apelike figures, stand harpers and storytellers, the *genus* that will supply the great poets who are to be found within the hall, and like them indicating by their mere presence that poets and makers are an indispensable part of Fame's array.

Far behind them, and apart, stand thousands of other nameless musicians, and, in yet another place, martial trumpeters. Professor Whiting has pointed out the resemblance to a scene in Renaud de Beaujeu's *Libeaus Descouneüs*, in which the hero is directed to a vast marble palace:[1]

> 'El front devant a mil fenestres,
> En cascun a un jogleor,
> Et tot sont de molt riche ator;
> Cascuns a divers estrument
> Et devant lui cierge ardent.
> De trestotes les armonies
> La molt doces melaudies.
> Tantost con venir vos verront
> Trestout viel vos salueront.'   (2818–26)

When he enters the hall he sees the jongleurs

> Sor les fenestres tos assis,
> Devant cascun un cierge espris;
> Et son estrument retenoit
> Cascuns itel con il l'avoit.
> L'un voit as fenestres harper,
> L'autre delés celui roter.

[1] See *Mod. Phil.* xxxi (1933), 196–8.

L'uns estive, l'autre viele,
Li autres gigle et calimele,
Et cante cler comme serainne;
Li autres la citole mainne,
Li uns entendoit au corner
Et l'autres au bien flahuter.
Li un notoient lais d'amor;
Sonnent tinbre, sonnent tabor,
Muses, salteres et fretel,
Et buisseines et moïnel,
Cascuns ovre de son mestier;   (2880–99)

Formally this represents a development of the catalogues of musical instruments that are a regular ingredient of scenes of merrymaking in Old French or Provençal romance; the wedding feast in *Flamenca* provides an early example. But Renaud de Beaujeu, for reasons that show a little more clearly in the English version of the tale, presents the scene as sinister: it strikes fear into the hero, and he lays a curse on the whole company. Chaucer's own tale of Sir Thopas (*CT*, B 2090) shows that he knew this romance, and he may well have taken some hints from it. But he has transferred the musicians and jongleurs from the inside to the outside of the hall; and his purposes are altogether more complex than the romance writer's. Since the palace he describes is that of Fame, and since it was described at the outset as standing

in so juste a place
That every soun mot to hit pace
Or what so comth fro any tonge,
Be hit rouned, red or songe,   (719–22)

he populates its walls with figures of those who *par excellence* represent the transmission of sound. It was from 'soun that comth of pype or harpe' that the eagle had taken his example for his soundwave theory (773); so these minstrels are not lay figures but actively making music, and Orpheus, pre-eminently, on a harp 'that souned bothe wel and sharpe' (1202); and because we now know from the eagle that all sound uttered on earth when it reaches this place 'wexeth lyk the same wight Which that the word in erthe spak' (1076–7) it is no surprise to find that these 'jogelours' and 'gestiours' are playing and telling tales. The phenomenon of sound and its multiplying quality has been the eagle's prime concern. As the element common to Rumour on the one hand and Reputation (fame) on the other, it has properly formed the subject of the second and central book; and at first these music makers seem to represent no more than, so to say, a sublimation of sound. Only when (much later) Fame's trumpeter produces his golden and brazen trumpets does the double appropriateness of the piping, harping, and clarioning become apparent. It is by such means that Fame spreads abroad men's glory or disgrace. Her house is a transmitter as well as a receiving centre; more strictly, the palace proper is a royal broadcasting station, the adjacent, but subordinate, house of twigs a kind of office for miscellaneous business.

In nothing does Chaucer depart further from the conventional array of instruments and gleemen than in choosing his representative musicians from several climes and ages. Orpheus and Arion (1203–5), exemplars of the poets as well as of the harpers of the antique world, provide a bridge from the versifiers ('gestioures', 1198) to the musicians proper; and the Breton Glasgerion (1208) is Orpheus's exact modern counterpart:

> He'd harpit a fish out o' saut water
> Or water out o' a stane.

Since Fame is by origin *Fama*, and in *Fama*'s hall falsehood mingled with truth (*Met.* xii. 54—a detail withheld when that source is first drawn on in Book Two), adjacent to these glorious crowders sit their counterfeits, 'di natura buone scimie' as Dante would have said, ll. 1212–13 being almost identical with *Inferno*, xxix. 139. The name Pseustis was known to Chaucer and all who learned 'gramere' from the ninth-century *Ecloga Theoduli*, a common school text which opens, as it happens, with a phrase from Ovid's *descriptio* of *Fama*. In this eclogue Pseustis indulges in a poetical contest with Alithia, relying on the ancient mythology while she (whose name is Truth) finds Scripture sufficient; Chaucer evidently thought of him as an historical character, and associated him etymologically (and archetypally) with fraud. Eventually Pseustis has to confess himself beaten. The parallel with the contest of Marsyas and Apollo is sufficiently close to account for the allusion to it in the lines that describe Marsyas as suffering for apelike and arrogant envy of the divine musician.[1] The diverse notes, some loud and clangorous, some lilting and pastoral (e.g. 1225), that issue from the pipes and shawms and clarions prefigure the sounds alternately sweet and harsh that Fame's trumpeter will blow on his more sonorous metal. But throughout the emphasis is on the multifarious multitudes—'alle maner of minstrales' (1198); all the clarioners that ever summoned Catalonia and Aragon to war (1247); gleemen beyond the stars of heaven for number (1254). The dream-faculty of increasing and multiplying figures Chaucer exploits in all his dream-poems: no one could reckon the creatures in the wood in the *Book of the Duchess* (427–41) or the birds in the *Parlia-*

[1] Chaucer has misread *Marsia* (*Paradiso*, i. 20) and so 'Marcia' appears as a woman (1229 f.).

ment (311–15). But here it is not simply dream experience that is imaged. These throngs of *simulacra* (see 1074–83) demonstrate the eagle's doctrine that

> every speche or noise or soun,
> Through his multiplicacioun,
> Thogh hit were pyped of a mouse,
> Moot nede come to Fames hous.   (783–6)

Since they have been coming hither since history began, small wonder that Chaucer concludes that the count would last 'fro hennes into domesday' (1284). But once here—so it seems to be implied—they become the servants and functionaries of that refinement of sound which is called Fame; their music becomes the echo of the song of praise that (as we are soon to learn) is perpetually sung before her throne.[1]

To add to the multitudes of musicians an equally varied array of jugglers, magicians, devisers of scenic illusions, and sorcerers of both sexes, may seem at first pointless or supererogatory. But their presence on the outer walls betokens some of the operations within just as surely as do the pipes and harps and trumpets. It is by these dubious arts—some harmless enough in themselves produce just such 'illusions' as the poet had prayed to be saved from (493)—that certain men 'have fame' (1276). Moreover, an element of japery and jugglery will prove to be part of Fame's character; her trumpeter will produce precisely the same effects as these when called on—a sound 'so ful of

---

[1] 1404–6. It is of some interest in this connexion that Boccaccio, when expounding the Narcissus myth (*De Gen. Deor.* vii. 59, 83 c) understands Echo (*quae nil dicit nisi post dictum*) as fame, who loves each mortal by whom she exists; many flee her and think little of her, looking for themselves in the waters of worldly pleasures. This curious interpretation is consistent with Boccaccio's own view that desire for fame is praiseworthy (ibid. xv. 13); cf p. 144 n. 1 below.

japes' that men go mad with laughing (1805–10). We are here being further alerted to the arbitrariness of Fame, who evidently takes no account of worth and makes a mock of those who expect her to be consistent. To clinch the *sentence* comes the allusion to Simon the Sorcerer (1274), with whose name we must associate not only the exemplary story of *Acts*, c. viii, but the ancient tradition that linked him with deviltry, bogus alchemy, and even Antichrist himself. He is here as the false trickster who tried to prove his magic powers by flying to heaven with the help of evil spirits, only to be brought low by St. Peter's prayers. Finally, the tregetour's contraction trick (1280–1) foreshadows—if that word may serve—the greatest 'ferly' of all: the opposite phenomenon of Fame's miraculous growth from less than a cubit to the height of the heavens. In sum, the environs of this gorgeous palace turn out to be the *kindly stede*, the natural *locus*, not only of all sound but of irrationality and confusion.

At length the dreamer gets to the gates of Fame's castle, no less rich and elaborate than the outworks (1302–6). If Chaucer drew from painters or other poets his general conception of the edifice, the details that he is now at pains to specify (beginning with the wall of magnifying beryl) are apparently of his own devising—at least of his own arranging—and so deserve the closer scrutiny. The gates are of gold—a further reminder that the castle (like Pluto's palace in *Sir Orfeo*, which it much resembles, and which Chaucer may well have known from the Auchinleck MS. of that poem) is 'out of this world'. But wonderfully carved as the gateway is,

> yit it was by aventure
> Ywrought, as often as by cure;   (1297–8)

once more the suggestion obtrudes that Fame is cousin to Fortune and crass casualty. This can scarcely be rationalized as a preview of Gothic art at its most flamboyant: it is more like the puzzling unexpectedness and fantasy of Gaudi's Sagrada Familia in Barcelona. Yet within the gatehouse with its rich vaulting and elaborate corbets the sense of craft and opulence still predominates. Here is the 'glistring foil' indeed. This entrance, by no means strait or narrow, deftly symbolizes the delight with which men seek renown.

By the same token, the blazonings and habiliments of the heralds and poursuivants who throng the inner court neatly epitomize the glamour of what had once been martial glory and had now congealed in forms and ceremonies. We remember that the poet who had begun his career in royal service kept a relish for heraldry all his life. But these figures richly clad in coat-armour so far surpass ordinary heralds—'somme corouned were as kinges' (1316)—that it takes time for the visitor to recognize them for what they are (1320); yet they are only the servants of the servants of Fame. Their splendid array, like their distribution of largesse, simply images the illusion that renown is purchaseable. To such trust in the power of heralds Gower witnesses when he describes the knight who 'for worschipe' makes 'many hastyf rodes'

> So that these heraldz on him crie,
> 'Vailant, vailant, lo, wher he goth!'
> And thanne he yifth hem gold and cloth,
> So that his fame mihte springe;
> (*CA*, iv. 1632–5)

Their claim that fame is 'oure owne gentil lady' is risible in its suggestion that they have any lien on her favour, yet plausible in so far as heralds and poursuivants would have the ordering of the trumpeters who would properly announce the appearance of such a queenly personage; though in fact when trumpets *are* blown for her (1590 ff.) it will be with scant regard for courtly decorum. The pomp of the poursuivants is touched with the Vainglory of which Gower says that it has always

> La cornette et la chalemelle,
> Pour solacer, u qu'il devient:
> Tous en parlont, 'Vei la q'il vient,
> Vei, la, qui sur tous mieulx revelle!'
>   (*Mirour de l'Omme*, 1263–6)

The immoderateness that attends the pursuit of Fame is at this point doubly though indirectly emphasized: first by the image of a book of heraldic arms twenty foot thick, and next by the picture of showers of gold nobles raining down on a floor already half a foot thick in gold (1345), in a hall gleaming with precious stones as closely set as the blades of grass in a meadow (1353); it is another feature reminiscent of the architectural fantasies assembled by Frankl: the *chambre de beauté* in the *Roman de Troie* (with its pillars of amber, jasper, onyx, and gagaret (= ?*gagâte*, jet), the tomb-chamber of Camilla in the *Énéas*, the grail temple in the *Titurel*; and these, however incredible, in turn remind us that there was some basis in fact for such wholesale use of precious stones: the Abbot Suger describes how he bought piles of them at bargain prices to adorn the high altar of St. Denis.[1] But Chaucer here introduces these splendours only to smile at the taste for them, striking thrice in ten lines that quizzical note that sounds at intervals throughout the poem. He could do,

---

[1] See E. Panofsky, *Abbot Suger* (Princeton, 1946), pp. 58–59. Among instances not noted by Frankl is the cloister in the M.E. *Land of Cokaygne*, with its pillars of turned crystal and bases and capitals of 'grene jaspe and rede corale' (l. 70).

he confesses, with a little of the stuff to line his purse
(a royal listener might take the hint); for the names of the
stones he refers us to the Lapidary, with the same dis‑
enchanted effect as he procured by his early casual reference
to Morpheus ('this god, that I of rede'); and finally a hint of
ennui—'hit were al to longe to rede the names...' (1354–5).

A plethora of rich ornament, then, in Fame's hall, but
in marked contrast to the crowded outside, few people:
'Ful moche prees of folk ther *nas*' (1358). To Fame's bright
throne of imperial ruby only a few of the aspirants (ap‑
parently) gain access, despite the claim of the heralds in the
outer court that she may be won by valour or 'richesse'.
The situation is in marked contrast to that in which Nature
is depicted in the *Parliament*: *her* only throne is a green
lawn, and *all* the birds are

> *prest* in here presence,
> To take hire dom and yeve hire audience.
> (*PF*, 307–8)

There, in Marvell's phrase, all things disposed are 'orderly
and near'—the true pattern of medieval Nature. The same
philosophy (likewise accepted by Marvell) informed the
medieval convention that made a beautiful woman
Nature's handiwork. And formally the *descriptio* of Fame
herself that now follows represents a bold conversion of
items from this familiar rhetorical *topos*. But of the typical
attributes of feminine beauty only one feature is allowed
her—the bright blonde hair

> that oundy was and crips,
> As burned gold hit shoon to see;   (1386–7)

in other words, it perfectly matched the materials of her
palace. This indication of femininity further establishes her
relationship to wavering Fortune, another *donna mobile*; it

also suggests the feminine nature of her power: the label on a popular Renaissance representation of Fame will read 'par son povoir comme *dame* exstimee'.[1] But otherwise it is the grotesque and strange unnaturalness of her figure that is stressed:

> never formed *by Nature*
> Nas swich another thing yseye   (1366–7)

The lustrous throne made out of a single gem—a notable materialization of the simple Virgilian phrase *luce sedet custos* (*Aen.* iv. 186, where *luce* means simply 'by day') itself embodies the disjunction between Art and Nature inasmuch as such a stone hardly belongs to the natural order any more than does its occupant. Fame herself is similarly enlarged and materialized from the three epithets Virgil had applied to *Fama* as Dido's betrayer: *monstrum horrendum, ingens.* None of this characterization had been apposite to the part played by 'wikke fame' in Book One, where Chaucer had followed Virgil only so far as to associate this malicious power with Dido's illhap, and where to depict it on the historiated murals would have been difficult. But now he can give body to Virgil's rhetoric without restraint. Even Virgil's *parva* becomes more precise when translated as 'less than a cubit' (itself an unusual term at this date); and whereas in the *Aeneid* *Fama*'s head is hidden in the clouds:

> mox sese attollit in auras
> ingrediturque solo et caput inter nubila condit
> > (*Aen.* iv. 176–7)

---

[1] See frontispiece. This tapestry is one of a series of six illustrating the Trionfi. Other copies are in New York and Brussels: for a full description and bibliography see *Charlemagne* [cat. of exhibition], Aix-la-Chapelle, 1965, it. 761.

The complete label reads: 'De terre vient la haulte renommee / Pour atropos et ses deux seurs renger / Car chastete elle a voulu venger / Par son povoir comme dame exstimee.'

for Chaucer *nubila* becomes the planetary heavens ('there as shynen sterres sevene', 1376). By this and other means Fame is made to resemble powers that far outsoar mere Rumour: namely—and the persistently ambiguous charac-ter of the whole poem should have prepared us for this paradox—Nature herself (whom both Brunetto Latini and Deguileville present as touching the stars with her head) and Boethius's Philosophy, *statura discretionis am-biguae*, who 'somtyme... constreinede and shronk hir selven lyk to the comune mesure of men, and sum tyme it semede that she touched the hevene with the heighte of hir heved; and whan she heef hir heved hyer she perced the selve hevene [*ipsum caelum*], so that the sighte of men looking was in ydel' (*De Cons. Phil.* I, pr. i, in Chaucer's trans-lation). This extraordinary elasticity, acceptable in such numinous figures as Philosophy, is a little harder to recon-cile with the conception of a goddess perpetually seated on a dais (1360 ff.); but the palace and even its pillars turn out to be endowed with the same astonishing power. When the visitor comes to one of the pillars he has to strain his neck to see its summit:

> Forwhy this halle, of which I rede,
> Was woxe on highte, lengthe and brede
> Wel more, by a thousand del
> Than hit was erst, that saugh I wel.   (1493–6)

Those tregetours on the outer walls, then, were but pale and paltry foreshadowings of the real magic within. This magic perhaps comes, like that of the Squire's Tale, from the land of Tartary, indeed from the very source that Livingston Lowes proposed as providing the setting of that tale—the Letter of Prester John, or rather from the insertion into the text of that famous apocryphal epistle that Zarncke called Interpolation D (*c.* 1250). There is described a *capella vitrea* which can stretch to any extent. However few or numerous the people in it this chapel remains full yet all have room. It can extend to infinity and then contract to hold no more than three.[1]

Variable in size, Chaucer's 'feminyne creature' is fixed in location. She therefore has no need of the *pernices alae*, the swift or 'preste winges' on which *Fama* flies in *Aeneid*, iv (and in *Troilus*); instead Chaucer puts partridge wings on her feet, as if, say editors, he had misread *pernicibus* as *perdicibus*; yet he may have found this chattering bird's wings an appropriate symbol.

However this may be, the alteration of Virgil's next figure is clearly deliberate. *Fama* is feathered, with eyes beneath the feathers, and for each feather there is an ear and a tongue:

> monstrum horrendum, ingens, cui quot sunt corpore
> plumae,
> tot vigiles oculi subter, mirabile dictu,
> tot linguae, totidem ora sonant, tot subrigit auris.
>
> (*Aen.* iv. 181–3)

This becomes:

> as fele eyen hadde she
> As fetheres upon foules be,
> Or weren on the bestes foure
> That Goddis trone gunne honoure,
> As John writ in th'Apocalips.
>
> . . . . .
>
> And, soth to tellen, also she
> Had also fele upstondyng eres
> And tonges, as on bestes heres.
>
> (1381–5; 1388–90)

[1] F. Zarncke, *Der Priester Johannes, Erste Abhandlungen, Koenigl. Gesellschaft der Wssenschaften, Abhandlungen, Phil.-hist. Kol.* vii (Leipzig, 1879); *Zweite Abb.*, viii (1883).

Apocalyptic allusions tinge more than one account of other-worldly experiences, and even some of the architectural fantasies that Frankl describes. So when Chaucer seats Fame on a ruby whilst making her sky-high he may well have expected us to think of that throne set up in heaven whose occupant was like a jasper and a sardine stone with a rainbow round about him like to an emerald (Rev. iv. 2–6).[1] Not identity of detail but a partial likeness of awesome, indeed beautiful, effect is involved. And the reverence accorded by the muses (the very muses invoked at l. 520) in their ceaseless praise before Fame's throne undoubtedly recalls the perpetual adoration of the four and twenty elders before the throne of the Lamb. These scriptural postures denote neither irreverent parody nor an arbitrary recasting of Fame's traditional character. They are simply a means of hypostasizing that appearance of glory which Chaucer here, and only here unqualifiedly, concedes to Fame—here, for the first time in the poem, identified with Renown (1406). By the same token there is no mistaking the verve and admiration that informs the whole passage beginning

> But, lord! the perrie and the richesse
> I saugh sitting on this goddesse!
> And, lord! the hevenish melodye
> Of songes ful of armonye;   (1393–6)

and there is no missing the resonance of the next two couplets:

---

[1] The references in the Apocalypse to such precious stones had been filled out at length by Fra Giacomino da Verona in his *De Jerusalem Celesti* (*c.* 1250) which devotes over twenty stanzas to them (see the editions by Esther Isopet May (London, 1930) and Mussafia, *Sitzungsberichte der Kais. Akad. W en* (1864)).

I herde aboute her trone ysonge
That al the paleys walles ronge!
So song the mighty Muse, she
That cleped is Caliope.

In the Vatican MS. of the *Libellus de imaginibus deorum* the nine Muses are pictured singing at the feet of Apollo; some such illustration may have prompted this scene.[1] Learning and the Arts are thus shown as the true and constant denizens of Fame's Palace; and we are ready for the suggestion—to be driven home as we consider the posture of the figures of poets and 'clerkes' on its supporting pillars—that renown involves a sort of subservience; Fame herself—Chaucer realizes at this precise point—is willing to bear the coats of arms of two famous men on her shoulders. The choice comes as no surprise to readers brought up on 'The British Grenadiers': Alexander and Hercules are supreme examples of what Fame can do for a man, given sufficient prowess to work upon: Alexander standing, we may suppose, for all the 'Neuf' Preux—hence his coat of arms would be familiar.[2] The heraldic reference means that we are to think of him as a chivalric hero, as Gower thinks of the Protesilaus to whose story he attaches the moral:

Lo, thus upon the worldes fame
Knyhthode hath ever yit be set.
(*CA*, iv. 1932-3; and see marginal gloss.)

Hercules was, in friar John Lathbury's words, *celo dignus*

[1] See J. Seznec, *The Survival of the Pagan Gods* (New York, 1953), pl. 68, and p. 178.
[2] They are plainly displayed (a lion rampant with halberd) in the illuminations in MS. Bodl. 264 (e.g. f. 421) and in MS. Bibl. Nat. fr. 12559, f. 125, repr. R. S. and L. H. Loomis, *Arthurian Legends in Medieval Art* (M.L.A., 1938), fig. 13.

propter facta famosa . . . propter fortitudinem.[1] Yet even here the
intermittent sardonic note is heard: Hercules' grim death by
Nessus' shirt (1414) being neither an instance of his forti-
tude nor an inducement to lesser men to strive for fame. The
link between this representative of the solitary hero and the
emperor who symbolizes martial power and kingly sway
was forged, it might be said, by Alexander himself when
'with al his hooste, proudly', as Lydgate, following Guido,
affirms (*Troy Book*, i. 603), he visited the pillars that
Hercules had laboured to set up at Gadez. The vault of the
hall itself is supported by columns on which stood (presumably within the 'tabernacles' beloved by designers and
artists of the period) the great poets and (since Clio is one
of the Muses) the great historians of the past; and perched
on smaller pillars are throngs of lesser writers (1514–16).
Chaucer's thoughts, as he himself has revealed (986), had
been on Alanus's 'Anteclaudian'; and at the very outset of
that work he would find developed the *topos* of a lofty
columned hall—the house of Nature, painted with the
figures of the famous: philosophers (Aristotle, Plato,
Cicero, Seneca); heroes (Alcides, Ulysses, Tytus, Turnus,
Hippolytus, *et al.*): names mostly drawn from Bernardus
Sylvestris's similar catalogue—which includes Chaucer's
Hercules, missing in Alanus; and poets: Virgil (*Virgilii
musa mendacia* [i.e. fictions] *multa colorat*), Ennius (*Priami
fortunas intonat*), and Maevius, whom he associates with
Alexander.[2] Alanus having thus indicated the pictorial

---

[1] Cit. B. Smalley, *English Friars and Antiquity*, p. 342. Boccaccio (*De Gen.
Deor.* xiii. 1) cites Rabanus's derivation of Hercules < heruncleos ('fame of
strong men'). In another tradition Hercules was granted fame by Zeus when
he permitted him to shoot the eagle gnawing at Prometheus's liver.

[2] See *Anticlaudianus*, i. 131–83, and Bossuat's notes thereto.

For an assemblage of figures of the great there is late-classical precedent in the
lararium of Alexander Severus: 'Vergilium autem Platonem poetarum vocabat,

possibilities in the theme of the famous dead when given the setting of a splendid hall, it is hardly surprising that Petrarch's *De viris illustribus* (for him this means Roman statesmen and generals) should have quickly prompted his patron Francesco il Vecchio da Carrara to commission frescoes representing them for his hall at Padua (*c.* 1370). These exist no longer, but from a codex that survives at Darmstadt it appears that the programme probably included a 'triumph' of Fame, in which the goddess was shown enthroned and wielding a sword.[1] Conceivably Chaucer saw the Paduan frescoes, or similar representations of Fame in manuscripts of Petrarch or of that part of Boccaccio's *Amorosa Visione* which describes *il trionfo di gloria*; but at most he could have owed to such sources a mere particularizing of the general conception as adumbrated in the *Anticlaudianus*. His exemplary figures turn out to be of his own choosing; whilst for their plastic representation we need seek for no closer analogue than the biblical or royal figures inhabiting many a Gothic porch or buttress or west front, from Strassburg to Wells.

Chaucer's capacity for devising such embodiments of literary subjects has already been amply evidenced in the first book of Fame. Now the renewed use of ecphrasis serves to indicate afresh that the Venus adored in the temple and the Fame worshipped in the palace are in a sense rival deities. His vigorous reconstruction in the

eiusque imaginem cum Ciceronis simulacro in secundo larario habuit, ubi et Achillis et magnorum virorum' (Lampridius, *Alex. Sev.*, cit. Comparetti, *Virgilio nel Medio Evo*, i. 59, where he also notes that Virgil's tomb came to be regarded as a temple).

[1] See Theodor E. Mommsen, *Medieval and Renaissance Studies* (ed. E. F. Rice, Jr., Ithaca, New York, 1959), pp. 154–5. Petrarch's text doubtless provided a welcome variation from the practice of decorating rooms with figures of the Nine Worthies or similar heroes.

Knight's Tale of the Temple of Mars first described by Statius was to show him seizing yet another opportunity of using this talent for the concrete picture. It is another of the gifts he shared with Dante; and it would make him especially responsive to Dante's representation of the third circle of Purgatory. There the sculpture of the Annunciation

> dinanzi a noi pareva sì verace
> quivi intagliato in un atto soave,
> che non sembiava imagine che tace.
> (*Purg.* x. 37–39)

(appeared before us carved so vividly in a gracious stance that it did not seem a dumb image [one would have sworn that it said *Ave*])

And in a memorable sculptural image the penitents who are expiating vainglory in the same circle appear bent like the corbel figures that squat as if to support a roof:

> Come per sostentar solaio o tetto,
> per mensola talvolta una figura
> si vede giunger le ginocchia a petto;
> (ibid. 130–2)

Chaucer's literary personages, who had promoted the fame of others rather than of themselves, and who are not victims of vanity, stand erect and exalted; but they too bear burdens on their shoulders—the subjects of their histories and poems. And the English poet had only to turn one page of the *Purgatorio* to find an apostrophe to fickle human glory in terms that in part resemble those of ll. 1140 ff., in part correspond to the lesson Fame herself is shortly to teach:

> O vanagloria dell'umane posse,
> com' poco verde in su la cima dura,
> se non è giunta dall' etati grosse!

. . . . . .

Non è il mondan romore altro che un fiato
  di vento, che or vien quinci ed or vien quindi,
  e muta nome, perchè muta lato.

Che fama avrai tu più, se vecchia scindi
  da te la carne, che se fossi morto
  innanzi che lasciassi il pappo e il dindi,
  pria che passin mill'anni? . . .

(*Purg.* xi. 91–93, 100–6)

(O the vanity of man's glory in his powers! For how brief a time does it flourish, if it be not vanquished by rude ages! . . . Worldly fame is nothing but a breath of wind, blowing hither and thither, changing name because it changes direction. If you put off your flesh when old rather than as a prattling infant, what difference will it make to your fame a thousand years hence?)

But against this powerful restatement of Boethius must be set Dante's unwavering belief in the long-lived glory of poetry, which is to be reaffirmed amid the great solemnities of Paradise itself:

O diva Pegasea, che gl' ingegni
  fai gloriosi, e rendili longevi,
  ed essi teco le cittadi e i regni . . .

(*Par.* xviii. 82–84)

(O goddess Pegasaean, who givest glory unto genius, and renderest it long life, as with thy aid doth it to cities and to realms.) (Wicksteed's rendering.)[1]

And Chaucer's immediate purpose is to represent this true glory in plastic form, singling out a succession of

---

[1] Dante himself did not always despise literary fame: in *De Monarchia*, I. i, he expresses the hope of being the first 'to win for my glory the palm of so great a prize'—though trusting more to divine light than to his own powers.

typical figures (which he associates with certain 'cities and realms'—Jerusalem, Thebes, Troy, Rome) in the way that Dante had introduced exemplary figures throughout the whole of the *Commedia*. Thus even this third book of Fame owes something of both its shape and its doctrine to 'the grete poete of Itaille'.

II

By his choice of the first figure for his pantheon Chaucer showed that his adaptation of earlier catalogues of Worthies was to be bold and free.[1] It is 'the Ebrayk Josephus, the olde' (1434) who heads the file. He may be taken as literary surrogate for the three Jewish members of the Neuf Preux—Joshua, David, Judas Maccabeus. The palace of the della Scala in Verona had been painted with scenes from the war of Jerusalem (doubtless involving Macca⁄beus) 'according as it is described by Josephus'.[2] But in

[1] See E. R. Curtius, *European Literature in the Latin Middle Ages* (tr. Trask), p. 260. Chaucer knew Dante's array of the ancient poets (*Inf.* iv). Lucan, Virgil, Statius, had figured in an eleventh⁄century list, and 'Theodulus', who appears in their company shortly afterwards, would be a precedent for introducing a modern author such as 'English Gaufride' (1470: see below). A vision in the twelfth⁄century Apocalypse of Golias gives the scholars and poets who were read in the schools—including Lucan, Virgil (making his bronze flies), Ovid, Persius, Statius, Terence: see F. J. E. Raby, *Secular Latin Poetry in the Middle Ages*, ii. 216. In the hey⁄day of scholasticism Henri d'Andeli, in *La Bataille des vii arts*, pictures Aristotle as 'crowned' by Persius, Juvenal, Horace, Lucan, Statius, Sedulius, Prosper of Aquitaine, Prudentius, Arator, 'Homer', and Terence (ll. 205–13.

Petrarch, of course, had introduced warrior⁄heroes as well as a medley of Greek and Roman philosophers, poets, orators, historians, legislators, physicians, and mathematicians into the *Trionfi*; the usual texts include (of those in Chaucer's list) Virgil, Homer, and Livy; and the Harleian MS. published by Prof. R. Weiss adds Statius and Lucan, Dares and Dictys, Josephus (and Egesippo, = Aegis, the abbreviator of Josephus), Dares, and Dictys ('Fra lor discordi è non e chi 'l ver cribri': cf. *Fame*, 1476 ff.).

[2] Vasari, *Vita di Vittore Scarpaccia*, quoted Theodor E. Mommsen, op. cit., p. 168. If Baudri de Bourgueil's description of some twelfth⁄century hangings

poetry the nearest precedent for the inclusion of the Jewish historian in any such list as Chaucer's appears to be in his friend Gower's *Confessio Amantis* (*c.* 1390) which names him along with nine less well-known historians who

> The ferste were of enditours
> Of old Cronique and ek auctours:
>   (*CA*, iv. 2411-12)

This couplet certainly suggests the reason why Chaucer, whose sequence of worthies is carefully chronological, begins with the narrator of biblical history. Josephus's prestige was of long standing, and his *Antiquities* neatly links the story of the Jews with that of Rome. The sheer antiquity of the events Josephus describes makes him 'of secte Saturnyn' (1432): as the oldest of the gods Saturn has to do with 'olde merveiles' (1442)—'he knew so manye of aventures olde', as Chaucer noted again elsewhere (*CT*, A. 2444). Lack-lustre lead is his proper metal. In Josephus's pillar it is mixed with iron since martial strife is his theme. Iron is Mars's metal—hence his temple in the Knight's Tale, as in Statius, is sustained by pillars of iron, 'bright and shene' (*CT*, A. 1994); but here the presence of lead sorts with the initial statement that the pillars 'shoon not ful cleer' (1422). They were of 'greet noblesse', although 'of no richesse' (1423-4); signifying that their occupants owed their place to real worth, not to the adventitious aids of 'craft' or 'largesse'. The massy pillars of enduring metal symbolize the permanence of their themes, and of their renown. 'The name of poet', Dante had said, 'is the one which most endures and honours

is to be trusted, Jewish history had early figured in mural decoration: he gives a list of scenes showing the Creation and the Flood, the Kings of Judah, Greek myths, and the Matter of Troy—and the Battle of Hastings (see F. J. E. Raby, *Christian Latin Poetry*, 282).

most.' Chaucer has translated this affirmation into particular terms, but qualified it by identifying writers with
the subjects they celebrate.

For Statius, the first figure named (though not the first
figure noticed: cf. 1453–4) after Josephus, a solid iron
column is especially appropriate since the Thebes whose
wars he celebrated was Mars's city. The column is 'painted'
all over with tiger's blood; a bizarre touch, bespeaking
Chaucer's minute study of the account of the iron temple
of Mars in *Thebaid*, vii, and denoting war of tigerish ferocity.
Statius probably owes his place, as he certainly owes his
appellation ('the Tholosan', 1460), to Dante, to whom
Statius revealed himself in Purgatory as a crypto-christian,
conscious of the early fame that had won him the myrtle
crown:

> 'col nome che più dura e più onora
> era io di là', rispose quello spirto,
> 'famoso assai, ma non con fede ancora.
> Tanto fu dolce mio vocale spirto,
> che' Tolosano, a sè mi trasse Roma.
> dove mertai le tempie ornar di mirto.
> Stazio la gente ancor di là mi noma;
> cantai di Tebe, e poi del grande Achille. . .'
>
> (*Purg.* xxi. 85–92)

The passage would attract Chaucer's notice as giving
Dante's view of the worth and lastingness of poetic
fame; and it will be seen from it that Chaucer follows
Dante not only in recognizing Statius's fame but in giving
Toulouse (instead of Naples) as his birthplace, and in
linking with the *Thebaid* his fragmentary *Achilleid*. But in
Chaucer Achilles figures not as 'great' ('grande'), but
as 'cruel' (1463). It is one of those dyslogistic notations
that creep into the description of Fame's hall even when

the poet seems most engrossed by its magnificence. It reflects the medieval tradition that Achilles' killing of the glorious (and favoured) Trojan hero Hector was a 'despitous' act;[1] it hints also that the Fame who can immortalize this Achilles is indiscriminate in her favours. It is because 'the gret Omer' (1466) was pro-Greek and anti-Trojan that he is now presented as the cause of contention between the historian-romancers in the hall who derive their themes from him: Dares and Dictys, Lollius and Guido delle Colonne (1467-76): the least statuesque of all the figures, since they are presented in active disputation. 'Who so that can', as Chaucer says elsewhere of the first of these pairs, 'may rede hem as they write'—except that Lollius never existed outside Horace. Dares, or rather the *Historia De Excidio Troiae* ascribed to him, comes inevitably in here, since its whole purpose (like, though to a less extent, that of 'Dictys') was to expose Homer's 'feignings' and 'to bear up Troy' (1472): that is, to justify the Trojans as against the Greeks—and to denigrate the Romans by defaming Aeneas. Guido (not yet the 'peevish and corrupt Guydo' of humanist criticism) stands appropriately alongside 'English Gaufride', for Geoffrey of Monmouth was Guido's almost only rival. It was Geoffrey's *Historia* that spread the tale of Brutus, eponymous founder of Britain, 'Brutus Albion', Troia Nova. Here for once Chaucer grows patriotic: the Trojans whom he had earlier to depict as persecuted by Juno (156, 201) are now vindicated by the place accorded to their poetic defenders in Fame's hall.

[1] Cf. *Tr.* v. 1555 ff. A thirteenth-century illustration of Benoit's *Roman de Troie* (fig. 70 in Margaret Scherer, *The Legends of Troy*, 1963) shows Achilles meanly spearing Hector through the buttock as he turns to seize a dead Greek's helm. See also Lydgate, *Troy Book*, iii, 5389-99, iv, 2784-90.

This allusion to the 'Troianysshe blood', recalling both the poem's opening scenes and the pro-Trojan sympathies that permeate them, leads naturally on to Virgil and to the Aeneas—here for the first and only time in Chaucer dubbed *pius*—whom Virgil had immortalized.[1] Virgil's pillar is faced with gleaming 'tin': for the outcome of the wars that Virgil celebrates was the founding of Rome the Great. 'Tin', moreover, was the metal of Jupiter—Aeneas's patron deity, as Chaucer had been at pains to make clear in his account of his wanderings in Book One.

Ovid, poet of Venus (and, as author of Dido's Epistle, conjoined previously with Virgil: 378–9) stands nearby on his pillar of copper, *cuprum* being Cyprian Venus's metal by etymology (hence it is the material of her temple in Boccaccio's *Teseida*); Lydgate conveniently moralizes it as indicating love's 'geeriness', since copper tarnishes to green, the colour of inconstancy (*Fall of Princes*, vii. 1239); Dante, mindful of Ovid's general artistic excellence, had put him in Limbo along with the other great poets of Antiquity here named. But it was pre-eminently as the poet of love that Ovid was regarded from the twelfth century onwards; and Chaucer's description of him as 'Venus clerke' appears to be a conscious variant of the appellative *doctor egregius* found in the famous disputation between knights and clerks, the burlesque council of Remiremont (*Concilium in Monte Romarici*). *Ars Amatoria* was widely used as a school text; the *Metamorphoses* as well as the *Heroides* were read as tales of love as well as of morality; and such was Ovid's prestige in this kind that erotic not to say lascivious poems (notably the *Ovidius puellarum*) of a much later date became attached to his

---

[1] In *Aen*. iii. 462 Helenus bids Aeneas *ingentem factis fer ad aethera Troiam*— 'By thy fatis large The fame of mekill Troy bair up to hevyn', as Douglas puts it.

name. His unrivalled and ever-increasing vogue (evidenced
in the 2,000-odd lines in the *Roman de la Rose* that—as
Chaucer doubtless detected—derived from him) is aptly
figured first in the image of his bearing up 'well' Love's
fame and secondly by his miracle-working power that
expands the limits of the hall a thousandfold. Love and
the poet of love are thus shown as sharing *Fama*'s own
magnifying quality.

'The grete poete, daun Lucan' (1499) stands here as
the author of the *Pharsalia*; his theme of civil strife requires
that his pillar should be of iron, bespeaking Mars—'open
werre . . . Contek, with blody knif, and sharp Manace'
(*CT*, A. 2002-3). To place on his shoulders

> As highe as that I mighte see,
> The fame of Julius and Pompee (1601-2)

is to indicate how great was the medieval prestige of his
epic. Dante had given him a similar eminence as one of
the four 'signori dell' altissimo canto Chi sopra gli altri,
com' aquila, vola' (*Inf.* iv. 94-96)—a form of reference that
may have affected Chaucer's presentation here. Both
poets had studied their Lucan closely; and the English
phrasing is especially appropriate in so far as it recalls
Pompey's own yearnings for glory, as expressed in
a passage that held Petrarch's attention.

By now the suggestion that the lastingness of such
worldly fame depends (as here it does almost literally) on
poets or historians and their choice of themes and heroes,
has been firmly implanted; and it is now seen to sort with
Chaucer's own preoccupation—notably in the frame-
prologues to each book—with the *ars poetriae*. This is the
still centre of the poem. The same power is predicated of

immortal verse that Dante had claimed for it in the *Com-media* when he invoked the Pegasean Muse who gives glory and long life to genius (see p. 137 above) and that Boccac-cio had asserted in the last two books of *De Genealogia Deorum* (*c.* 1363). If Chaucer anywhere departs from earlier medieval assumptions about the status of poets it is here. Yet he does so silently, almost imperceptibly, as if without knowing it, certainly without ostentation. And even here, as C. S. Lewis remarked, 'in the last resort it is the fame they give—the fame of Aeneas, not of Virgil—that really matters'.[1] Chaucer guards at once, moreover, against the danger of implying that the elect are fixed and few in number. For alongside Lucan stand the many other 'clerkes That writen of Romes mighty werkes' (1503-4); amongst whom he must be reckoning such historians as Livy, Suetonius, and the Valerius Maximus of *De factis et dictis memorabilibus*— a title that might itself be construed as giving its author a claim to a place.

For final proof of poetic power stands Claudian, on the sulphurous pillar that denotes the infernal setting of his *De Raptu Proserpinae*: the pagan mythology owes its very survival in the Middle Ages to such poets. As belonging to the pre-Christian world (and being different from the planetary influences associated with Venus, Saturn, Mars, *et al.*) Pluto and Proserpina are fittingly associated with hell and 'the derke pyne' (1512). Thus yet again the sense of Fame's splendour is diminished—here by a glimpse of other powers, sinister and sad presences that now appear to have been adumbrated in those highly dubious 'Phito-

---

[1] *The Discarded Image* (Cambridge, 1964), p. 213. Petrarch thought of his poetry as bringing fame to his lady (*Rime*, ciii, ll. 12-13). But Boccaccio speaks of a true poet as living by fame after death (*Life of Dante*, tr. Wicksteed, p. 24).

nesses, charmeresses, olde wicches, sorceresses' (1262) who
denote the false and the crafty as contrasted with the
'honest' harpers, trumpeters, and gleemen inhabiting the
pinnacles of the castle wall. And at this stage we are fully
prepared to believe that 'hit a ful confus matere Were *al*
the gestes for to here' (1517–18), even though the recording
of these gesta had earned many an (unnamed) writer
a place in the hall. In a piquant simile Chaucer compares
them in multitude to the rooks' nests that crowd on the
tops of trees (1516). It signalizes both the conclusion of
the catalogue and a change of tone and topic. Instead of
poets serenely placed on seemingly eternal pillars we see
rooks busily cawing on windy elms. And even as the poet
cranes up his neck to look at them he hears 'a noise
aprochen blive' (1521). A company of all sorts and conditions of men bursts in with the murmurous bustle of a
hive, shattering finally the museum calm suggested by the
contemplation of poets and historians dead and gone.
These two simple yet vivid similes of the crowded rookery
and the swarming hive (the latter Milton was to use in the
grand mock-heroic manner at the end of the first book of
Paradise Lost) prefigure the action, ambience, and atmosphere of the remainder of the poem.

CHAPTER IV

Fortune's Sister

There was suyng to the Quene of Fame;
He plucked hym backe, and he went afore;
Nay, holde thy tunge, quod another, let me have the name;
Make roume, sayd another, ye prese all to sore;
Some sayd, Holde thy peas, thou getest here no more.
A thowsande thowsande I sawe on a plumpe:
With that I harde the noyse of a trumpe—
SKELTON, *The Garland of Laurel*

FROM the static and the statuesque, then, from the solid pillars that imply a permanence of Fame we pass in a trice to the miscellaneous throng of her living suppliants, still subjects of that fortune which is as mutable as the visiting moon (1531). And now at last the poet shows his hand. When once this 'ilke noble quene' (1535) breaks into speech and addresses her earthly devotees she reveals herself as arbitrary and whimsically perverse. Nowhere in the poem is his comment so deliberate or so emphatic:

But this I seye yow, *trewely*,
What hir cause was I niste:
For of this folk ful wel I wiste
They hadde good fame eche deserved
Although they were diversly served;
Right as hir suster, Dame Fortune,
Is wont to serven in comune.   (1542–8)

In short, the motives prompting Fame are beyond human divination (1543). Even so Virgil had said of Fortune, when addressing Dante as a representative human inquirer about her operations: 'Your knowledge cannot under-stand her' (*Inf.* vii. 85). Justly is Fame described as Fortune's own sister; she shares Fortune's duplicity, symbolized by her one auspicious and one drooping eye, or by a countenance now fair, now fierce. Fame, we have lately learnt, is the 'kindely place' of sound (840-2); but 'sound is caused by change, and has no fixed and stable existence . . . but actually *consists in* a movement or change'.[1] Hence we can expect from Fame no actions that will satisfy the human desire for consistency or stability. Terrestrial glory must be represented as irrationally bestowed since, as Gower says,

> The world,* as of his propre kynde
> Was ever untrewe, and as the blynde
> Improprelich he demeth fame.
> He blameth that is noght to blame
> And preiseth that is noght to preise.
> Thus whan he schal the thinges peise,
> Ther is deceipte in his balance
> And al is that the variance
> Of ous, that scholde us betre avise . . .
>   (*Confessio Amantis*, Prol. 535-43)
>   * i.e. the man of the world.

How suggestive was this association of Fame and Fortune may be seen from Shakespeare's picturing of Fortune (instead of Fame) enthroned as a sovereign lady on a steep

---

[1] St. Thomas Aquinas, Commentary on Aristotle, *De Anima*, ed. cit., pp. 279-80. H. R. Patch assembles other instances of the association of Fame and Fortune in *The Goddess Fortuna in Medieval Literature* (Camb., Mass., 1927), p. 110, n. 3. A less direct linkage is found in the *Ayenbite of Inwyt* (a close translation of *Le Somme le Roi*) in which the wheel of Fortune ('hap') is com-pared to a windmill that wafts to man all the twelve winds of 'idle bliss' and turns his thoughts 'to his guod los[fame] and to his prayzinges þet overal uleth' (E.E.T.S. ed., p. 24, ll. 26 ff.).

and slippery mount, the base of which is thronged with 'all kind of natures' (cf. 'alleskinnes condiciouns', 1530) 'that labour on the bosom of this sphere to propagate their states'; one man may be 'beckoned from the rest', but 'Fortune in her shift and change of mood' soon spurns down her late-beloved.[1]

It is all of a piece with this view of 'the green gods of fame and chance' that the first group of suppliants, when refused the full and immediate reward they had claimed ('graunte us *now* good fame', 1555), should be denied any reason ('cause', 1563) for the refusal. But their plea for 'ful recompensacioun' (1557) pertinently recalls the eagle's words when he promised the very glimpse of Fame that Chaucer is here being vouchsafed. Jove 'through his grace' (i.e. his unmerited favour) had willed that the poet should be thus cheered 'in some recompensacioun' for his 'causeless' service to an indifferent Cupid (664–8). Comparison of the two passages makes clear the difference between Fame's operations and divine Jove's. Jove renders to a man in some sort at least according to his deeds, and rewards labour beyond desert. Fame positively delights in thwarting those anxious for her favour. These first petitioners are not unlike Dido's first category of lovers— those who wanted 'fame In magnifying of [their] name' (305): their good works (1558) are not done for goodness' sake. But to draw any moral from this is no part of Fame's character.

A desire for 'good fame' now begins to appear as a weakness to which the worthiest men (all this company 'seyden sooth', 1552) are susceptible. Few are indifferent to the length or tenor of their future obituary, or find

---

[1] *Timon of Athens*, I. i. 64–86. Cf. *T. Andron.* II. i. 126–7: 'The emperor's court is like the house of Fame / The palace full of tongues, of eyes, and ears.'

Benefacite et mutuum date, nihil inde sperantes anything less than a counsel of perfection. Only men of St. Paul's kind can attain to complete disregard of earthly reward and minister *per gloriam et ignobilitatem, per infamiam et bonam famam* (2 Cor. vi. 8); though his words and attitude inevitably affected all medieval thought on 'good fame' (Chaucer's phrase precisely renders *bona fama*)—and weighed with Dante when considering the permanence of his own poetry after there had been displayed to him 'l' anime che son di fama note'.[1]

To be to dumb forgetfulness a prey is more, Gray suggests, than the meanest peasant can bear. Yet such is the fate decreed for those overzealous for earthly fame:

> No wight shal speke of yow, ywis,
> Good ne harm, ne that ne this! (1565–6)

And it is not till they are 'out of the story' that Fame summons her trumpeter. With this summons (1568) comes another turn of speed; and the sense of an imperious personality which has been implanted by Fame's first decree is vividly confirmed by the sharp phrasing of her message to Aeolus, god of winds, and her threat to the messenger '. . . up peyne to be blind anoon' (1570). Once before in the poem a cruel goddess, Juno, had called on Aeolus to blow 'hideously and high' (cf. 204–5 and 1599). It was in accord with the same Juno's purpose (as against Venus's) that Virgil's *Fama* had spread the news of Dido's secret espousals. And there is something Junoesque about Chaucer's Fame. She summons her nameless messenger in just the same haughty style that Juno adopts in the *Book of the Duchess* to rouse her messenger to Morpheus: 'Go now faste, and hie the blyve'—and flying fast

[1] Cf. C. G. Hardie in *Traditio*, xix (1963), 281, 288.

to the dark valley he cries 'O, ho, awak anoon' (*BD,* 179),
just as Fame's emissary 'gan fast crye "rys up and faste hye"'
(1592). Here is the same sense of bustle, the same touch
of the termagant. There is no unbridgeable gulf between
such deities and the Wife of Bath, who indeed did not
think of herself as alien to the mythological world, claiming
that she could get the better of Argus himself (*CT,* D. 360).

To make Aeolus Fame's trumpeter was a fine stroke,
not least because it amply justifies the presence of the
eagle's earlier discourse on the nature of sound. The germ
of the conception is perhaps to be found in Virgil's
association of Aeolus and Juno (*Aen.* i. 64). Certainly
Chaucer's account of Aeolus's cave and of his manner of
controlling the winds derives directly from the *Aeneid*:

> hic vasto rex Aeolus antro
> luctantis ventos tempestatesque sonoras
> imperio premit ac vinclis et carcere frenat.
> illi indignantes magno cum murmure montis
> circum claustra fremunt;   (i. 52–56)
>
> (. . . quhair Eolus the Kyng
> In gowstie cavis, the wyndis lowde quhisling,
> And braithlie tempestis by his power refrenis,
> In bandis hard schet in presoun constrenis;)

Virgil, however, locates the cave not in Thrace but in the
Liparian wilds of Sicily, 'full of cavernys, with bryntstan
blawand and brynand onder the erd', as Douglas com-
mented. The association with Thrace may be due to a passage in Horace which is actually quoted by Servius in his
Commentary on *Aen.* i. 57, and so probably came under
Chaucer's eye:

> Jam veris comites, quae mare temperant
> Impellunt animae lintea Thracie;
>   (*Od.* IV. xii. 1–2)

But the mythographers had followed Virgil, and from his locating the forge of Vulcan likewise on a Sicilian island (*Aen.* viii. 416) had deduced a close nexus between Vulcan (the blacksmith) and Aeolus (the worker of bellows), so that they came to be thought of as partners in business. Whether Chaucer knew of this association or not (and Nequam, Boccaccio, and the author of the *Libellus de imaginibus deorum* evidently did), his Aeolus certainly plays something of the same subordinate, banausic role in Fame's temple that his Vulcan had in Venus's (see p. 21); which serves to strengthen one's impression that the ecphrases of the two temples are deliberately juxtaposed.

Long ago Lounsbury plausibly suggested that it was one of the mythographers, known to him as Albricus Philosophus, who first gave to Aeolus the two trumpets that he bears in Chaucer. 'Albricus' (*alias* 'Mythographus Tertius Vaticanus') thus depicts him:

. . . stabat enim in antro, linea veste indutus et praecinctus, tenens sub pedibus flabia [bellows], instrumenta fabrilia. *In manu autem utraque tenebat cornua*; quae ori admovens eo sufflere [= sufflare] et ab utroque cornuum sex ventos emittere videbatur.[1]

In fact at least one pre-Chaucerian mythographer, John Ridevall, repeats this description; and an early-fifteenth-century manuscript of his *Fulgentius metaforalis* has a picture of Aeolus with the trumpet horns at his lips and his feet on the bellows.[2] Thereafter allusions to Aeolus's 'bugles'

---

[1] *Scriptores rerum mythicarum latini tres . . . nuper reperti*, ed. G. H. Bode (Celle, 1834), p. 170. For 'Alb[e]ricus' see E. Rathbone in *Medieval and Renaissance Studies*, i (1941), 35–38; B. Smalley, op. cit., p. 111, *Cahiers de Civilisation Médiévale*, 31–32 (1965), 431; and J. Engels in *Vivarium*, ii (1964), 118.

[2] The miniature, with adjacent text, is reproduced by Panofsky, *Studies in Iconology*, pl. xiii, fig. 24 (and see p. 45). The virgilian associations are reflected

become common. Already in the *psychomachia* that closes
the *Anticlaudianus Fama* has a trumpet (*cornu*) with which
she bellows forth her own praises (*sue preconia laudis
Intonat: Acl.* ix. 139–40); and a pair of trumpets were to
become a regular Renaissance attributes of Fame; they are
a feature of Biard's famous statue, now in the Louvre, and
of Strozzi's later painting.[1] It is unlikely that Chaucer was
the first to assign such instruments to the goddess, yet
amongst his contemporaries his friend John Gower
appears to have been the only writer to make the association. In the *Mirour de l'omme*, after a long account of the
rise and decline of ancient kingdoms, Gower introduces,
to point the moral, an address to Fortune, variable and
(literally) double-faced—one visage smiles, the other weeps.
Everything pertaining to her seems more changeable than
the wind; now she is peaceable, now 'venteuse'—an
epithet sufficient in itself to link her with Aeolus. Still
more relevant is the allegation that 'Whoso seeks thy company and magnifies and praises thee, to them thou dost
despite, whilst those that abhor and shun thee thou settest
up in high honour' (*Mirour*, 22120 ff.). This is the very
fashion in which Chaucer's Fame serves some of her

in that part of the drawing which shows Juno placing a crown on Aeolus's head
quia Juno suum regnum dedisse fingebatur.

For angels with trumps who apparently represent four personified winds
(cf. Rev. vii. 1) see *Cahiers*, 31–32 (cit. n. 1 above), 361–2; but it is unlikely
that Chaucer had any scriptural associations in mind at this point.

[1] A version of Biard's stature ascribed to Guillaume Bertelot stands,
appropriately enough, near Strozzi's painting in the National Gallery, London.
The two 'trumps' are differentiated in both, the lower one held by the naked
goddess of the statue being more like a short pipe, whilst Strozzi's pleasant-
featured and fully dressed figure (also with wings) has a dull-coloured horn in
one hand, a gleaming one in the other (cf. next note). Whether the same
significance attaches to the upward- and downward-pointing orifices of the
trumpet on the tapestry of the frontispiece (cf. the elephants' trunks) is doubtful.

suppliants. Gower's Fortune, moreover, (and here one thinks of Odin's birds in the Prose Edda) has two hand-maids who fly faster than swallows, and bear news of her court which is one day good, the next day bad. The first, flying to noble folk of Renommée, gives them 'favelles d'honneur', whilst the second is defaming them. And as they fly they sound their diverse tidings through great horns suspended from their necks:

> Cist duy par tout u sont volant
> Chascune entour son coll pendant
> Porte un grant corn, dont ton message
> Par les paiis s'en vont cornant.
> Mais entrechange nepourqant
> Sovent faisont de leur cornage,
> Car Renomé, q'ier vassellage
> Cornoit, huy change son langage,
> Et d'autre corn s'en vait sufflant,
> Q'est de misere et de hontage:
> Sique de toy puet estre sage
> Sur terre nul qui soit vivant.
> He, comme Fortune par tout vole,
> Or est tressage, ore est tresfole,
> Or est doulcette, ore est amere,
> Ores est commune et ore est sole.
>   (*Mirour*, 22141-56)

Emblems of Fortune's variance, even these trumps are interchangeable; while the speed of their flight indicates the fleetingness of Fame: 'Where now is the Rome of the Caesars?' It is *derere*—a ruin (22160).

In short, Gower treats the followers of Fortune exactly as Chaucer treats the petitioners of Fame, indeed he depicts Fortune as arbiter of Fame. And it seems likely that Chaucer, accustomed to pairing Fame and 'windy'

Fortune, read his friend's *Mirour* and saw that the two
horns Gower gives to Fortune could be equated with the
two horns traditionally borne by Aeolus, and saw too
that they would be fit attributes for Fame the deceitful
and double-mouthed.[1]

It is illustrative of the 'hooking' power of Chaucer's
poetic memory that he develops these allusions by a
reference to Virgil. For he forthwith introduces as Aeolus's
trumpet-bearer the classical Triton, whose appearance here
is evidently due to the poet's study of *Aeneid*, vi. 164 ff.—
a passage he has previously drawn on at l. 1243. Virgil
there calls Misenus 'the son of Aeolus' (*Aeolides*) because,
as Boccaccio says (*De Gen. Deor.* xiii. c. 23), the two operate
in a similar way: 'quia ventorum Eolus deus dicitur, quasi
eorum auctor, sic a similitudine operis Misenus eius dicitur
filius'; 'the sound of a trumpet being produced by the impulse of breath through a tube [it is the point made by the
eagle when explaining sound, 765 ff.], just as wind is air
sent forth by pipes and caves in the earth'. If Misenus could
be identified with Aeolus on these grounds, with equal
ease could Triton, the son of Neptune and Amphitryon,
whose wreathed conch or horn Chaucer would know
about from Ovid:

> bucina, quae medio concepit ubi aera ponto,
> litora voce replet sub utroque jacentia Phoebo.
> (*Met.* i. 337–8)

---

[1] Lydgate refers to the two trumpets (and to the house of fame) in *Fall of
Princes*, i. st. 16–17. Patch (op. cit., p. 112) notes that Pierre Michault (*fl. c.*
1460) in 'La Danse aux Aveugles' gives *Eur* a silver trumpet and a high pillar,
Maleur 'au plus bas du trosne' a worn wooden one.

Milton's 'double-mouthed' (*Samson Agonistes*, 970–1; see p. 157) is clearly a
variant of Chaucer's 'doubletongued' (*CT*, I. 570 (§ 46); cf. Wiclif. *New
Test.* 1 Tim. iii. 8).

The notion that Triton should carry the trumpets, like a man serving a master, is as novel as it is diverting—like the inessential, almost whimsical episode of ll. 1598–1601, where Aeolus, in the act of obeying the messenger, remits his pressure on the winds; as he releases one of them it blows all the clouds away; a picture recalling a well-known incident in the early adventures of Ulysses but here possibly suggested by a simile in *Purgatorio*, xxviii (a canto adapted by Chaucer in the *Parliament*, 182 ff.), where the breezes blowing through the 'paradiso terrestre' are compared to the sough of the wind in the Ravenna pines 'quand' Eolo Scirocco fuor discioglie'.[1]

By the time the second company of suppliants arrive Triton and Aeolus have taken up their stations at Fame's feet. Like the first group, these candidates demand fame as their desert (1613), but they expect it 'in honour of gentilesse' (1611)—as due, that is, to their rank, ancestry, and breeding. The phrase is crucial, recalling as it does in the first place the poursuivants of 'riche folke' (1322) who had addressed 'our oune gentil lady Fame' (1311) as if identifying her with their own 'gentility'; and in the second place Philosophy's warning about glory in Boethius: 'And yif that folk han geten hem thonk or

---

[1] *Purg.* xxviii. 21. In Skelton's *Garland of Laurel* (which represents Chaucer as promising Skelton a place in the court 'of noble Fame before the quenes grace') Aeolus appears primarily as Fame's trumpeter. He blows a martial 'bararag' and summons the poets 'with a full terrible blast'—but also drives clouds together 'like drifts of snow' (cf. *Fame*, 1600).

The young Milton, a professed follower of Chaucer (hence the Tityrus of *Mansus*, 34) has Fame herself carry, at Jove's behest, a sonorous trumpet of Italian bronze to spread reports of Gunpowder Plot:

Dextra tubam gestat Temesæo ex ære sonoram.
.   .   .   .   .   .
Ambiguas voces, incertaque murmura spargit . . .
(*In Quintum Nov.* 207–12)

preysinge [*gloria*] by hir desertes, what thing hath thilke
prys eched or encresed to the conscience of wyse folk, that
mesuren hir good, nat by the rumours of the people, but
by the soothfastnesse of conscience ? Yif [Philosophy adds
later] the name of gentilesse be referred to renoun and
cleernesse of linage, thanne is gentil name but a foreine
thing [*aliena*] . . . that comth of the deserte of ancestres'
(*De Cons. Phil.* iii, pr. vi; Chaucer's version). That
Chaucer took this to heart is evident from the emphatic
restatement of the doctrine in the Wife of Bath's Tale:

> But for ye speken of swich gentilesse
> As is descended out of old richesse
> That therfor sholden ye be gentil men—
> Swich arrogance is nat worth an hen.
>   (*CT*, D. 1109-12)

And the Wife proceeds to impeach the very folk who
would count ancestral 'gentilesse' sufficient warrant for
fame:

> For gentilesse nis but renomee
> Of thyn auncestres for hir high bountee;
> Which is a straunge thing [cf. *aliena*] to thy persone.
> Thy gentilesse cometh fro god allone
> Than cometh our verray gentilesse of grace,
> It was nothing biquethe us with our place
>   (1159-64; cf. Boethius, op. cit. iii. m. vi)

Her 'strawe for your gentilesse!' is just what Fame's reply
amounts to: 'As thryve I, ye shal fayle' (1615). Both are
dramatic expressions of sober Philosophy's judgement:
'Foreine gentilesse maketh the nat gentil'. These gentles,
like their predecessors, have insisted on immediate recognition ('*now*', 1611)—which merely provokes Fame to
decree for them a reputation actually worse than they

deserved. If this apparently harsh decree reveals her malignance, concomitantly it exposes the folly of those who mix their claim to renown, however just it be, with pride. And it is stinking pride that is suggested by the foul swart smoke which now issues from Aeolus's trumpet of 'light slander' (1625). In accordance with the law of sound as expounded earlier (809 ff.), the further this slander spreads, the greater and the worse it grows. To describe the effect Chaucer for once crams five colour words (two of them first found here) into a single short line—'blak, blo, grenish, swartish, reed' (1647)—then adds the crowning touch that 'hit stank as the pit of helle'—appropriately enough since it issued from a blackened trumpet 'fouler than the devil' (1638). The proud were traditionally the devil's trumpeters, inhaling (says *Ancrene Wisse*) the breath of worldly praise ('hereword'); they 'makieþ noise and lud dream'—like the heralds of 1322—'to schawin hare orhel' ('to display their pride').[1]

The proud, then, whatever their real merits, are prey to Fortune. 'What *aventures*', exclaims the poet, 'han these sory creatures!' (1632). Fame, if not like Fortune 'double-faced', is 'double-mouthed' and—here, as in *Samson Agonistes*—'with contrary blast proclaims most deeds'. It is only by equating Fame with this same Fortune as regards

---

[1] *Ancrene Wisse*, C.C.C.C. M.S., ed. Tolkien, p. 109. Gower uses a similar figure in describing the 'proude vice' of Avantance (Boasting) which 'his oghne Herald is' and

> Hath thilke wynd in his office,
> Which thurgh the blastes that he bloweth
> The mannes fame he overthroweth
> Of vertu, which scholde elles springe
> Into the worldes knowlechinge;
> Bot he fordoth it alto sore.
>
> (*CA*, i. 2410–15)

unpredictability that we can account for her completely different treatment of the third company: those who are equally conscious of their deservings but are rewarded by having their reputation spread to the ends of the earth. Yet again this is not mere perversity on Fame's part; their claim is plausible and does not depend on rank or the virtue of their ancestors; they ask no more than that their fame should be known '*right as it is*' (1664). If they get more than their deserts it is because the exaggerative nature of Fame is necessarily present in good report as in bad (. . . *quam nuntia veri*: *Aen.* iv. 188). The notes of Laud, the golden trumpet, linger on the air, bearing the fragrance of balm and roses and suggesting, in contrast to the sulphurous blast from Lipara, Zephirus's 'swete breth': an altogether happy image of the relish that attends popular recognition of one's virtues.

Thus far each company has knelt submissively if not adoringly at Fame's dais. The different posture of the fourth group at once signalizes their different view of her. Standing upright in line, they claim that they have done with their might what their hands found to do, but for virtue's sake alone ('for bountee', 1698) and are professedly content to be as they had never been. Yet they address Fame as 'lady briht', and there is a touch of ostentation in their stance. Fame takes their plea at its face value, and for once the trumpets are silent. This sort of virtue does indeed die without memorial as often as do the deeds done out of desire for glory. 'The deed becomes unprais'd, the man at least.'

The fifth group, like the third, represents a subtle variation on its immediate predecessor. Here the longing for anonymity is intense and deep. It brings this 'route' to their knees as they tersely express their *contemptum mundi*:

'they yeven noght a leek for Fame' (1708). Their contemplative lives are hid in God. They thus bear to group
four the relation that Langland's contemplative Dobet
bears to his active Dowel. At this point Chaucer seems
once again to have 'thought on Anteclaudian'. For when
in Alanus's poem Prudence has outsoared the stellar
hierarchy she comes to what in Dante is the heaven of
Contemplatives (*Paradiso*, xxi–xxii). Here, says Alanus—

> Hic habitat quem vita deum virtusque beatum
> fecit et in terris meruit sibi nomen Olimpi,
> corpore terrenus, celestis mente, caducus
> carne, Deus vita, vivens divinitus, extra
> terrenum sapiens, intus divina repensans.
> *Quem non erexit fastus, non gloria rerum,*
> non mundi deiectus amor, non lubrica fregit
> luxuries, non luxus opum, non amor habendi
> succendit, non livor edax, non anxia fedat
> pestis avaricie, non *laudis ceca cupido*,
> sed pocius donavit eum Prudencia, mundi
> contemptus rerum paupertas, arctaque victus
> regula, despectus carnis, deiectio vite . . .
>
> (*Anticlaudianus*, v. 443–55)

(Here dwell those whom . . . neither pride not vainglory puffed
up nor worldly desire nor dangerous lechery crushed; the
ostentation of wealth, the greed of gain did not inflame them;
devouring envy and the troublous disease of avarice left them
untouched. Not for them the blind passion for praise. Rather
Prudence bestowed on them scorn for the world, spiritual
poverty, a meagre way of living, a despised kind of life)

—a conclusion that brings sharply to mind Chaucer's own
conclusion to his greatest work: '. . . This blisful regne may
men purchace by poverte espiritueel and the glorie by
lowenesse' (*CT*, *ad fin.*). His verve and gusto never blinded

him to the transcendent worth of the spiritual life; and if
there is nothing of Dante's sublimity in his treatment of it
in this poem, there is something of Dante's precedent
and example. Certainly the contemplatives whom Dante
instances perfectly illustrate the paradox of Fame's next
decree. Womanishly incensed by the group's despisal of
her favour, she bids Aeolus proclaim on his golden
trumpet their praises to the ends of the earth. The notes
sound softly yet incisively ('kenely', 1725); and 'atte laste
hit was *on lofte*' (1726)—more than is said of any of the
other trumpet calls. Their fame, then, and theirs alone,
reaches and rests in that heaven where Dante had found
those exemplary contemplatives St. Benedict and St. Peter
Damian—both in earthly life raised to eminence against
their will, both owing their after-fame likewise to their very
contempt for it.[1] That Fame follows those who flee her,
just as she runs from those who covet her, is a paradox
beyond Milton's reach. When his Christ argues that 'if
there be in glory aught of good' it may be attained 'by
deeds of peace, by wisdom eminent, by patience, tem-
perance', his only instances are Socrates and Job (*Paradise
Regain'd*, iii. 90 ff.); all other glory is 'vain'.

With fame in love, represented by group six, we turn to
a wholly different theme—or rather turn back to the
episode (Dido's reproaches, 305 ff.) with which 'fame'
makes its entry into the poem. Essentially idle—and in this
contrasting with their predecessors—these suppliants hope
to pass as zealous though refusing to put themselves out

---

[1] *Par.* xxi. 61–xxii. 45. They thus present an antithesis to the treacherous
Antenor who in *Inf.* xxxii (91–94), when Dante says 'caro esser ti puote ... se
domandi fama / ch'io metta il nome tuo tra l' altre note' ('if thou seek fame it may
please thee that I include thy name with the rest'), replies: 'Del contrario ho io
brama' ('it is the opposite that I yearn for'). [See Additional Notes, p. 188.]

for any woman: their concern is simply for reputation. There is a touch here of Guillaume de Lorris's *Oiseuse*, and a glimpse of his *Roman's* world of courtoisie which had its braggarts as well as its *sirvientes*. The very language is '*courtoise*'—'Mercy, lady dere', they cry (1730). But only the language. The stance is that of the young/men/about/ town, alluded to in *Troilus*, who 'han won Love with to greet an ese'; and indeed 'oure grete ese' is their prime con/ cern (1753). No company asks more of Fame, yet to none is she more compliant. But their reward is hollow. For all the glory they acquire so cheaply, 'they gon in full bad lese': the bucolic image (there are to be more such) deftly punctures their pretensions. Fame's assent to them really represents no more than a translation of Boethius's *Gloria vero quam fallax, quam turpis est!* . . .—'But glorie, how deceivable and how foul is it ofte!. . . For manye han had ful greet renown by the fals opinion of the poeple, and what thing may ben thought fouler [*turpius*] than swiche preysinge?' (*De Cons. Phil.* iii, pr. vi, *ad init.*). Milton was to make the same point, though with respect to the fame of emperors, not lovers: it is but 'the peoples praise, false glory', attri/ buted 'To things not glorious, men not worthy of Fame' (*Paradise Regain'd*, iii. 48, 69–70). In marked disjunction comes the contemptuous dismissal of the seventh company. Though identical with the sixth in their pleas and pre/ tensions, they are first denounced and mocked in good Billingsgate, and then exposed as the frauds they essentially are. Fame's mode of action here once more reveals her composite nature, as previously hinted at in the external decoration of her castle, with its counterfeit musicians aping the true. If she allows some braggadocios to impose on the populace, she sees to it that others shall be ridiculed and made, like real apes, a spectacle to men (1805–10).

Aeolus's black trumpet plays for once a mocking tune—
but plays it as loudly as the winds blow through hell. The
simile is not taken at random; it is the same blast that
bellows in Dante's second circle, the stormy place, void of
light,

> che muggia, come far mar per tempesta
> se da contrari venti è combattuto.
>
> (*Inf.* v. 29 ff.)

and it makes part of the thunderous 'grete sound' (actually
compared to a tempest, 1036) that the poet had heard
before he reached Fame's castle.

Groups eight and nine present the last permutations on
Fame's pattern. First the notoriously wicked are refused
Fame, though the goddess, by her 'Al be ther in me no
iustyce' (1820), implies that it would not be discordant
with her nature to grant it. Grant it she does, in fact, to
their successors, those who are not only evil but find their
sole delight in doing evil, and positively rejoice that the
world should know it. For such men the black trump is to
sound, but the effect is hardly what they had intended.
Their spokesman and prototype is the villain who names
himself only as the destroyer of the temple of Isidis; coming
last in the line of the named figures who stand in the hall,
he stands in a kind of parodic antithesis to Alexander
(1413). And there is a further connexion. History relates
that he set fire to the temple (of Artemis, and at Ephesus,
not 'in Athenes') on the night that Alexander was born.
The Ephesians decreed that thereafter his very name
(Herostratus) should be unspoken—and it survives in one
source only. Chaucer's choice of him thus appears to be
made with deeply ironical intent. The man who most
brazenly aimed at malicious reputation does indeed gain

it, but gains also, quite literally, the loss of his 'name'. He wears a bell (and 'swiche a belle', 1841, suggests that it was a large one) on the tippet of his (fool's) cap; so he is to be associated with the 'gestiours' on the pinnacles of the castle (1198). The mere motion of his head helps to proclaim his folly.

And now the spectator, as if he has had more than enough, turns to go. Renown, oblivion, ill-repute have been shown to depend on Fame's whim as much as on desert. When a new interlocutor amiably inquires his name and errand he pointedly abjures any desire to beg favour of the goddess, and even declines to answer the question. 'No wight', he says, playing on the senses of *name*, '[shall] have my name in hand' (1877); he will not give even his thoughts as hostages to fortune, but will stick to his poet's last:

'For what I drye or what I thinke,
I wol myselven al hit drinke,
Certein, for the more part,
As ferforth as I can myn art.' (1879–82)

This neatly concludes the action within the hall. But it also illuminates the poet's earlier disavowal of any desire to display his art poetical 'for maistrye' (1094). As earlier he had shrunk from the thought of being 'stellified', so now he is not so presumptuous as to think that his power to describe a vision of Fame's temple gives him a claim to a place in it. On the other hand he avoids pretentiously despising Fame. No poet who puts his name to his work can do that without hypocrisy. So Dante, though modifying the ambitions set forth in the first chapter of *De Monarchia*, refrains from completely disavowing desire for poetic glory. And Chaucer, in the very act of distancing himself from the

famous writers of old time, modestly yet clearly affirms his
belief in poetic worth. It is this belief that motivates his
quest, not an itch to see whether his own name will be
written in the perdurable ice of Fame's hill.[1] It is for new
poetic *matière* (his request further reminds us) that he has
professedly been brought here—for some new and wonderful 'tidings'—if not about love, about 'swiche thinges
glade'. Of Fame's suppliants he had known in a general
way 'sith that firste I hadde wit' (which is to say at least
since he had read Boethius); all that he has so far learnt
beyond this is 'hir condicioun' (1904). 'So you don't count
this as wonder enough?', says, in effect, his anonymous
questioner. 'Come this way then, and you'll hear more.'

[1] But it is of some interest that this is the only poem in which Chaucer the
narrator identifies himself; indeed it is the first English narrative poem—as
distinct from a chronicle or exegetical work—in which the author so names
himself.

CHAPTER V

Whirling Wicker

Rumor next, and Chance
And Tumult and Confusion, all imbroil'd.
And Discord with a thousand various mouths.
Paradise Lost, ii. 965–7

Mille fores aditusque patent totidemque fenestrae,
Amplaque per tenues translucent atria muros;
Excitat hic varios plebs agglomerata susurros;
Qualiter instrepitant circum mulctralia bombis
Agmina muscarum, aut texto per ovilia iunco . . .
MILTON, *In Quintum Nov.* 175–9

(A thousand doors and approaches stand wide open and as many
windows, and through the thin walls glimmer the spacious rooms.
A vulgar throng gives rise to murmurings like those made by
swarms of flies buzzing round milk pails or in rush-woven
sheepcotes)

ONE effect of the crisp dialogue that precedes the poet's
departure from the castle is to lend perspective to the scenes
enacted within it. It is now evident that the climax of the
action lies elsewhere. And it is time to remember that his
first guide had found him deficient not only in love-tidings
but in knowledge of his 'verray neyghebores' at his door-
step. For at the gate of the castle he sees 'faste by' its
workaday counterpart, a suburb in the strict sense, standing
outside (and just below) the castle wall as huts of thatch
and wattle stood outside the medieval *castellum* yet were
part of it, if the perishable part. It is a single vast house of
woven wattle and in perpetual motion, creaking as if
spun round by the wind. In its simple and impermanent
materials there is a distinct suggestion of the primitive.

Primumque furcis erectis et virgulis interpositis luto parietes texerunt, says Vitruvius ('at the beginning they put up rough spars, interwove them with twigs, and finished the walls with mud').[1] So Virgil, contrasting the elegant Capitol of his own day and its distant predecessor in Aeneas's time, speaks of it as 'now roofed with gold, then thatched with thorn' (*Aen*. viii. 348).

But such hints or suggestions hardly constitute precedents; and for several features of this house of twigs precedents or parallels are hard to find. Taken in order of importance the apparently novel features are:

(i) Its precise location—in a valley, immediately below the hill of Fame, where it is 'founded to endure Whil that it list to Aventure' (1981-2)—i.e. built to last for just so long as Chance allows. Here the association with Aventure provides a clue. For Alanus's house of Fortune is similarly placed: part is firmly set on the mountain-top (see p. 106 above), part clings to the mountain-foot, on the verge of collapse:

> Rupis in abrupto suspensa minansque ruinam,
> Fortune domus in preceps descendit . . .
> (*Anticlaudianus*, viii. 1-2)

The 'ruyne' associated with Rumour (1974) must be given the material sense suggested by these lines—*Casum tanquam lapsura minatur*, adds Alanus. All the mean and impermanent features in the antiphrasis that has earlier contributed to the palace of Fame, Chaucer has reserved for Rumour.

(ii) The style and material of the building. It is the elaborate construction that first excites the visitor's wonder, reflected as that wonder is in the comparison with Daedalus's

---

[1] Quoted by Panofsky, op. cit., p. 44.

labyrinth. The essential point of likeness is the intricacy of each structure: as the *multiplex domus* that Daedalus built for Minos had its blind and deceptive passages, a 'conflicting maze of divers winding paths' (*variarum ambage viarum*: *Met.* viii. 161), so this house is skilfully and deliberately built ('queynteliche ywroughte') to provide innumerable entrances, vents, and windows in the interstices of the wickerwork. For Chaucer, as for Virgil and Ovid, Daedalus was *ingenio fabrae celeberrimus artis* (*Met.* viii. 159); and besides the labyrinth and the wings that 'changed the laws of Nature' (ibid. 189) he built, *ut fama est*—'as report has it'—a temple to Apollo. So at least says Virgil, and describes how he set it up at Cumae near the cave of the *horrenda Sibylla* after his illfated flight, and depicted on its portal the whole legend of the minotaur:

> hic labor ille domus et inextricabilis error;
> magnum reginae sed enim miseratus amorem
> Dædalus, ipse dolos tecti ambagasque resolvit;
> (*Aen.* vi. 27–29)

Thus for the Middle Ages Daedalus was preeminently the cunning builder and inventor. Alanus refers to him as the former when describing the attributes of Prudence: *ut Dedalus erigit arces* (*Anticlaudianus*, ii. 352). As the latter he has already appeared in *Fame*, being the wretch whose craft brought disaster on his son (919)—an allusion which must make us chary of interpreting the present allusion as extolling his creative genius *à la* James Joyce. *Domus Dedali* (1928) recalls Mirk's 'hous of dadull', and may well have a dyslogistic sense.[1] Moreover the effect of the intricate cagelike basketwork is to suggest again a lack of solidity. Even

---

[1] 'My howse ys an hous of oresons. But . . . now hit ys made an hous of dadull and of whisperyng and rownyng': Mirk, *Festial* (ed. Erbe), p. 279.

so does Alanus (as seen already) underline the contrast between the two sides of Fortune's house: the one gleaming with gold and adorned with a lofty roof, the other rubbishy and full of holes:

> resplendet pars una domus; pars altera vili
> materie deiecta jacet. Pars ista superbit
> culmine sublimi, pars illa fatiscit hiatu.
>   (*Acl.* viii. 10–12)

And Jean de Meun had not only elaborated this com-parison but deepened the disparity, specifying mud walls thinner than the palm of his hand, roof of straw, cracks and holes 'more than five hundred thousand':

> S'est toute couverte de chaume
>
> .   .   .   .   .
>
> E pourfendue de crevaces
> En plus de cinc cenz mile places.
>   (*Roman de la Rose*, 6108–14)[1]

But Jean was still concerned to depict the reverse, and reverses, of Fortune. Chaucer represents the house as of daedal art because, though he has separated Fame from Rumour, he recognizes that no great gulf divides them. So his house of Rumour, though accommodating all sorts and conditions of men, and primitive in its materials, is no decayed and dirty hovel; and one detail that in the *Roman* is merely realistic Chaucer invests with both a practical and a symbolic purpose. The French poet roofs the rude structure with straw like a penthouse. Such a hut-ment would generally be built of wattle, so that osier or

---

[1] See further H. R. Patch, *The Goddess Fortuna*, pp. 127–8 and pl. 7. In Spenser the house of Pride, in which Lucifer sits gorgeously enthroned, is craftily built and covered in gold foil, but rests on a sandy foundation 'and all the hinderparts, that few could spie / Were ruinous and old' (*Faerie Queene*, I. iv. 4–5).

willow ('timber of no strengthe', 1980)[1] came to be a proverbial synonym for fragility, witness the Wife of Bath:

> Whoso that buildeth his hous al of salwes
>
> . . . . .
>
> Is worthy to ben hanged on the galwes.
>
> (*CT*, D. 655 ff.)

Whatever the commentators say, Chaucer would not need
to wander in Wales or Ireland to find such dwellings.
They were a part of any rural scene, and remained so till
Milton pictured the plebeian rout of *Fama* as buzzing like
the flies round the shepherds' huts *texta iunco*. Such sheds
might indeed be 'shapen lyk a cage' (1985)—or at least
like a beehive. Evidently we must think of a skip or cage
suspended from the battlements of the castle and so vast
that the eagle, when the time comes (2030), can easily
enter through one of the apertures. It is tempting, though
fruitless, to speculate whether the image was suggested to
Chaucer by the cage in which Alexander's birds bore him
up through the aerial regions; we can certainly read it as
a preparative for the reentry of the eagleconductor into
the action of the poem: for the next moment Chaucer
catches sight of his bird 'perched hye upon a stoon' (1991).
Only a bird in flight could offer to show him the inside of
the cage—'So faste hit whirleth, lo, aboute'.

(iii) Though a whirling movement might easily be
postulated of light basketwork hanging in the wind—
'as with the wynd wavys the wickir' is Dunbar's symbol
for 'warldis vanite' in his 'Lament for the Makers'—the
emphasis on the speed of the rotation suggests something
supernatural, and scholars have reasonably compared the
revolving castles of medieval romance. In the Welsh *Fled*

---

[1] The term 'wicker' is first recorded in *OED* in connexion with straw used
for thatching: *Cal. Doc. Scot.* 1336.

Bricrend, for example, Cúroí's fortress revolves as fast as a millstone after he departs for the skies; and *Arthur of Little Britain* (Lord Berner's version of a composite French text that obviously embodies traditional motifs) includes an account of a similar phenomenon.[1] Yet of itself 'whirl-ing' has associations far less arcane. It is the action regularly predicated of the great wheel of Fortune. And what more natural, since Fame and Fortune are kin, than that the annex to Fame's palace should share this attribute of Fortune's wheel? It is of this wheel that the *Apocalypsis Goliae* says

> Incedit quilibet cum rota mobili,
> dum mentis volvitur axe volubili
> et circumflectitur voto mutabili
> intus sequitur rotam a simili. (121–4)

Paintings in manuscripts and murals had made the figure a commonplace long before Chaucer wrote his balades 'de visage sanz peinture'; in the first of which Fortune *whirls* up and down (11)—just as she does in the Chaucerian *Romaunt* (4362; no equivalent in the *Roman de la Rose*); in the (almost equally Chaucerian) *Kingis Quair* (st. 165); in the contemporary alliterative *Morte Arthure* ('abowte cho whirlide a whele with her whitte hondes', 3260)—and in many a Tudor poem. The juxtaposition of Fortune's moving wheel and the hut of wretched straw and gaping roof, representing her reversals, in the miniature reproduced by Patch (op. cit., pl. 7) now takes on a fuller significance.

This rude structure is the fit haunt of half-baked stories, the rumours and travellers' tales that flit in and out of it—raw material on which the poets who gain permanent place in the house of Fame have to work, as different from

[1] Cf. Roger Sherman Loomis, *Wales and the Arthurian Legend* (Cardiff, 1956), p. 137, and *Arthur of Little Britain*, ed. of 1816, p. 143.

the finished *opus* as is the 'swough' and 'chirking' of the basket-house from the piping and the melody that sounded from the castle walls. By the same token the noise that issues from within the house is not trumpet-toned but like the jarring sound made as a siege-engine hurls its stone (1933-4).

Other differences between the castle and its annex deserve notice:

(i) The shaded side of the hill of ice, the castle's walls, roof, floor thickly plated with gold, its massy pillars, all give the effect of permanence and stability; and we are specifically told that Fame is 'perpetually ystalled' (1364) on her carbuncle throne. The basket house whirls round 'so swift as thought' (1924). The sudden change of tempo is characteristic of the poem as a whole: against the intellectual excitement of the Prologue has been set the torpor of Morpheus; against the slow movement round the temple of Venus the *prestissimo* of the eagle's descent. (And it is the eagle's lessons on sound laws that we must now recall, for they explain why all noises, all 'tidings', great and small, reach these ever-open doors.)

(ii) Fame's hall is not only spacious but indefinitely expansive (1375, 1494-6). The house of tidings has a measured length of sixty miles—and is crammed to bursting; the visitor can scarcely find room to stand (2041-2); to open one's mouth is to speak into a neighbour's ear (2044-5).

(iii) Fame holds imperial court, has servants at command, and receives profoundest homage. In the house there is no order, no hierarchy, not even a porter. All is constant jostling, plebeian fashion. The throng is noisy, miscellaneous, hurried; shipmen, couriers, pardoners, pilgrims (2120-30). It is like stepping from the decorum of dooms and audiences in the great hall of Westminster to the crowded streets of Thames-side. And Ben Jonson was to localize such a house of fame or report in a London 'shop' where 'all do meet'

> To taste the *cornucopiae* of her rumours,
> Which she, the mother of sport, pleaseth to scatter
> Among the vulgar.
>   (*The Staple of News*, III. ii. 115–20)

(iv) Fame's hall resounds with heavenly melodies sung in her honour (1395 ff.). The house of tidings is 'full of rounings and of jangles' (1960). The discord represents nothing less than the thousand shocks that flesh is heir to. Here is none of the formalized presentation of Fame's suppliants as they wish to be seen, but the raw and random miscellaneity of life, with all its changes and chances.

The cataloguing of this farrago of humanity is not the less vivid because it has literary congeners. Of one of these the rhetorical shape of the long asyndesis (1960–76) irresistibly reminds us, and the likeness is not fortuitous. In the Knight's Tale Chaucer displays just such a catalogue at even greater length when setting down the deeds pictured in the temple of Mars:

> Ther saugh I first the derke imagining
> Of Felonye, and the compassing,
> The cruel Ire, reed as any glede,
> The pikepurs, and the pale Drede,
>   (*CT*, A. 1995–8)

and so on, through memorable images of the 'dyvers transmutaciouns' and 'dyvers accidents' only alluded to in general terms in *Fame*. Hate, strife, fear, war, fire, famine, 'ruin', death, all spoken of in this house of tidings, have their abstract equivalents in Mars's Ire, Drede, Contek,

Manace, Meschance, 'armed Compleint, Outhees and fiers Outrage'; and alongside are their grim embodiments— pickpurse, butcher, weaponsmith, doomed huntsman and charioteer, and that 'smilere with the knife under the cloke' whom Shakespeare was to place in Rumour's train when he painted her full of slanderous tongues, a toy for 'the still-discordant wavering multitude'. Others of the tidings find similar equivalents (and in a similar rhetorical pattern) in Saturn's self-portrait in the same Tale:

> Myn is the strangling and hanging by the throte;
> The murmure and the cherles rebelling,
> The groining and the prive empoisoning
>
> .   .   .   .   .
>
> Myn is the ruine of the hye halles
>
> .   .   .   .   .
>
> And myne be the maladies colde,
> The derke tresons and the castes olde . . .
>
> (*CT*, A. 2458–68)

The ultimate source of the picture of Mars's temple is undoubtedly the *descriptio* in Statius's *Thebaid*, vii. 40 ff., from which Boccaccio took his pattern for the fairer temples of Venus and Diana in his *Teseida*. Chaucer's remodelling of these (in the Knight's Tale, and in the *Parliament*) involves some significant divergences from Boccaccio; but each temple retains its distinctive attributes—whereas in *Fame* inconsistent and irreconcilable elements, attributes of several different deities, Peace (Venus), War (Mars), Jealousy and Folly (Venus again), Dread (Mars), Famine (Saturn)—are all, like the other contraries (good government and bad, love and hate, rest and labour), piled pell-mell on each other. With the qualities, fates, and fortunes that astrology assigned to the houses of the planetary deities Chaucer was thoroughly familiar. But he is at present

concerned to hint that in the house of rumours and tidings
no such astrological pattern could be traced.

In so doing he is enlarging and enriching the *fons et
origo* of the whole of this third book—that seminal passage
in Ovid which has already provided the primary account
of Fame's habitation (p. 71 above). As he bisects the
classical (and Virgilian) concept of *Fama* into 'Fame' and
'Rumour', so he bisects Ovid's description, reserving for
the house of twigs the features that in Ovid pertain to
a house of sounding brass:

> innumerosque aditus ac mille foramina tectis
> addidit, et nullis inclusit limina portis;
> nocte dieque patent; tota est aere sonanti;
> tota fremit, vocesque refert iteratque quod audit;
> nulla quies intus, nullaque silentia parte,
> nec tamen est clamor, sed parvae murmura vocis . . .
>
> . . . . .
>
> atria turba tenet: veniunt leve vulgus, euntque;
> mixtaque cum veris passim commenta vagantur
> milia rumorum; confusaque verba volutant;
> e quibus hi vacuas implent sermonibus aures;
> hi narrata ferunt alio, mensuraque ficti
> crescit, et auditis aliquid novus adjicit auctor.
> illic Credulitas, illic temerarius Error
> vanaque Laetitia est consternatique Timores,
> Seditioque repens, dubioque auctore Susurri.
> ipsa [sc. Fama] quid in caelo rerum pelagoque geratur
> et tellure, videt; totumque inquirit in orbem.
>
> (*Met.* xii. 44–63)

> To this capacious bowre
> Innumerable waies conduct; no way
> Barr'd up; the doors stand open night and day.
> All built of ringing brasse, throughout resounds:
> Things heard, reports, and every word rebounds,

No rest within, no silence: yet the noyse
Not loud, but like the murmuring of a voice.

.   .   .   .   .

Hither the idle Vulgar come and goe;
Millions of Rumors wander to and fro;
Lyes mixt with truths, in words that vary still.
Of these, with news unknowing eares Some fill;
Some carry tales; all in the telling growes;
And every Author addes to what he knowes.
Here dwells rash Error, light Credulity,
Dejected Feare, and vainly grounded Joy.
New rais'd Sedition, secret Whisperings
Of unknown Authors, and of doubtful things.
All done in Heaven, Earth, Ocean, Fame surviews;
And through the ample world inquires of newes.

(Sandys)

The chief likenesses to the house of twigs—the thousand
apertures, countless ever-open entrances, the crowds, the
noise, the magnifying of report—are patent. It is only when
he comes to the personified abstractions of Credulity, Error,
Joy, and so forth that Chaucer makes significant changes,
extending the list till it is ten times as long as Ovid's.
Credulitas he includes as Trust, *Timores* as Dread (1971);
but *Laetitia* is excluded, like *Seditio*, though Saturn's
'cherles rebelling' offers an apt (and topical) translation
of the latter—and the *Susurri* have become 'tidings' as
well as 'whisperings'. But Chaucer's own list begins with
subjects not even hinted at by Ovid, except in so far as his
Fama spreads news (of the Grecian fleet's approach) that
spells ruin for Troy. 'Of werre, of pees, of mariages' is the
opening line in Chaucer's list. They are the concerns of
Mars, Venus, and (in the Knight's Tale at least) Diana.
But there quickly follows a breathless panoramic survey

of almost every aspect of human life and fortune, involving, if we think in astrological terms, all of the gods, but in no ordered sequence or coherence. For 'qualme of folk and eek of bestes' (1968) Saturn is responsible: 'Myn loking is the fader of pestilence', he says in the Knight's Tale— but also for 'ruyne' (1974: 'myn is the ruin of the hye walles'). Mars stands for strife (1964) but also for fire (1976: hence the burning of the 'shippes hoppesteres' pictured in his temple in the Knight's Tale). The love that belongs to Venus (1964) is separated by six lines from her other attributes (Jealousy, Winning, Richesse, Folly: cf. *CT*, A. 1925 ff.). By such means the effect of *confusa verba* is so strengthened that we are already prepared to look beyond the rhetorical *tour de force* and the literary pattern to the unsorted actualities of every-day which will bulk larger as the poem spins to its close.

There remain some miscellaneous, novel, and memorable features of the cage: the 'gigges and chirkinges' (1942-3), the porterless doors, the total absence of ease (1956). They all appear to be suggested by, or rather to suggest—by their very dissimilarity—that other dwelling in a valley, which Chaucer alludes to, otiosely at first sight, in the first book of this poem; namely, the cave of Morpheus. Sleep's house (as Ovid and Chaucer describe it) is the exact antithesis to the abode of 'tidings'. It is doorless, so that there shall be *no* 'chirking' ('there is no door which mai charke', as Gower puts it); and porterless (as well as windowless) for the same reason (*custos in limine nullus*)—whereas in the cage a porter would delay the entrants (1954). Instead of ceaseless activity (1956) there is languorous repose (*muta quies habitat*); instead of 'rouninges and of iangles', not a single sound (*non . . . humanaeve sonum reddunt convicia linguae*). It is the quiet shapes of dreams, not the roof-holes that are there numbered by the thousand (*Met.* xi. 633) and that lie thick 'as leves been on trees' (*Fame*, 1946; cf. *quot . . . silva gerit frondes*: *Met.* xi. 615). The closing scenes of the poem are brought by means of such antitheses to stand in ironical contrast to the opening prayer to the god of sleep and rest. For the prayer has been answered by a dream that reaches its climax in scenes of harsh noise and busy clamour.

The re-entry of the eagle into the action at this point likewise serves to complete the frame of the poem, inasmuch as it recalls the real purpose of the aerial journey (2007). The bird at once intimates that the end is near: 'Joves wol thee solace Fynally' (2008–9). Now the poet can talk to him, and of him, like an old friend; he is '*myn egle*' now (1900), just as Douglas's interlocutress, after he has passed through the Palace of Honour, becomes 'my nymph'. But the eagle at once reminds the poet that it is merely the emissary of Jove, the deity to whom both Fame and Fortune must be subject. The poet himself is now openly presented for the first time as a victim of this Fortune, who

> hath maad amis
> The frot [? *l.* fruit *or* rote] of al thyn hertes reste
> Languisshe and eek in point to breste;   (2016–18)

It is due, then, to the Fortune of whose whirling wheel this cage is reminiscent, that the poet had served Cupid and Venus 'withoute guerdoun ever yit' (619). Jove has already offered him partial 'solace'—by those scenes of *natura naturans* that had led him to cry 'moche is thy might and thy noblesse'; by the marvels of Fame's palace; and by the sight of the hardly less wonderful house of twigs. And the poet has sensed that in this last he may hear 'that leef me were, or that I wente' (1999). The bird now confirms that he has indeed come to the chief source of 'tidings'. No gloss on this word is vouchsafed, but its constant repetition constrains us to dwell on it. Clearly it is more specific than 'talk', less literary than *novella*. 'Tales' alone will serve to convey the fourteenth-century range of meaning, since it touches on 'anecdote' or 'story' at one extreme, 'report' or 'rumour' at the other. And 'tales' is surely the clue that we should follow in this *labyrynthus Daedali*. The introvert and bookish writer of love-poetry—so the eagle had hinted on his first appearance—must lift his eyes to the world and the people about him, those neighbours from Cheapside that he might meet at any inn. And, taking charge once more, the bird thrusts him—much as Africanus in the *Parliament* thrusts him into Nature's park—into the midst of a 'congregacioun of folk' as various and as numerous as the bird-kind in that same park. The poet himself, it appears, cannot of his own power or volition enter these domains that represent new 'matere of to write', new sources of poetic inspiration. He needs, no less than Dante though he soars in lower flight, the help of that divine virtue for which both poets had invoked Apollo.

But once the eagle has again 'hente [him] up bitwene his toon' (2028) and set him down within the cage, the case is altered. Inside one is no longer conscious of the *perpetuum mobile*—'methoghte hit stente' (2031); and what had seemed from without a mere medley of noises becomes a kind of macrocosm wherein each human kind 'doth straight its own resemblance find'. The poet, that is, when divinely guided, can reach the still centre of this turning world, can watch the whole process of a tale's gestation. Man is a tale-telling animal; and the manner of his tale-bearing—this the whole unfolding of the poem implies—is almost as wonderful as the operations of Nature herself.

For no tale remains as it began. Just as sound is magnified when spread abroad, like a circle on water, so story, the concatenation of meaningful sounds, spread primarily by word of mouth, is magnified and 'improved' as it passes from one man to another. The image used to express this 'increase' provides yet another Virgilian reminiscence and yet another instance of Chaucerian economy:

> And that encresing ever mo
> As fyr is wont to quikke and go
> From a sparke spronge amis,
> Til al a citee brent up is. (2077–80)

This is a concise variant of the simile that Virgil uses to describe the oral report (*fama*) of Dido's death and the clamour it occasioned: a passage that Chaucer omitted from his paraphrase in Book One, but did not forget:

> concussam bacchatur Fama per urbem.
> lamentis gemituque et femineo ululatu
> tecta fremunt, resonat magnis plangoribus aether,
> *non aliter quam si immissis ruat hostibus omnis*
> *Karthago aut antiqua Tyros, flammaeque furentes*
> *culmina perque hominum volvantur perque deorum.*
> (*Aen.* iv. 666–71)

> (. . . Nane other wys than thocht takyn and doun bet
> War al Cartage, and with ennemys ourset,
> Or than that natyre cite the town of Tyre,
> And furyus flambe, kendillit and byrnand schyre,
> Spreding fro thak to thak, baith but and ben . . .)

This then is the house of Rumour, and Rumour, in Shakespeare's image, 'doth double, like the sound and echo' everything committed to it (*2 Henry IV*, III. i. 97). Thus even literal truth, once retailed, changes its nature, and history takes on the character of fiction. The 'lesing' and the 'sad sothsawe' that struggle to get through the narrow aperture together (2089–109) become tenaciously intertwined. Here the *persona* of Virgilian Fame is fragmented into winged tale-bearers interlocking as they struggle in a microcosmic *psychomachia*. The poet began with a meditation on the degree of truth and falsehood in dreams, traditionally associated with poetic creation. He passed to the tale of Dido, indissolubly linked by Virgil to the operations of winged report *tam ficti pravique tenax quam nuntia veri*— a line that is here anthropomorphized into the image of sworn brotherhood (2100–1). He concludes with an insight into the very nature of poetic narrative, that genre of which he was to become the first and finest master.

The cage is like a hive, buzzing with tales—some destined to perish on men's lips, some to be given permanence in literature (thus we may gloss 2110–14), according to whether Fame favours the poets who reshape them. The brief re-entry of Aeolus at this point, and in a new role, serves to relate these activities—or at least to show that there is a relation—to Fame, goddess of the pillared hall of poets. He blows the 'wenged wondres' about like birds tossed by a gale (2119–20)—the significance of the comparison of the daedal house to a wind-blown cage is now apparent—and, as if to demonstrate a variant of the law asserted at 1674 ff., they embody the talk of the tale-bearers with whom the cage is crammed: seamen and pilgrims, messengers and pardoners—the traditional and representative spreaders of stories 'tall' and otherwise. Here in little is that 'full tide of human existence' that Dr. Johnson delighted to watch in motion at Charing Cross. It is out of this gallimaufry that the professionals pick their fictional wares. The true inwardness of the dreamer's aerial tour, hitherto but dimly disclosed or sensed, seems to dawn on him while we watch him scurrying to and fro 'me for to pleye and for to lere' (2133). Suddenly he has perceived that as well as the world of physical phenomena which the eagle has expounded there is a human world of untapped wonder; that the marvel of the law of sound has its earthly, human counterpart in the law of 'encres' in story. To say that Fame gives increase and duration to story is to say, in effect, that this is what worthy poets, 'clerks', and minstrels do; which is the reason why they adorn the walls of her palace and the pillars of her hall. She who in Virgil has 'as many tongues as a bird has feathers' gives to story her own *pernices alae*; and the winged wonders form a last reminder that the whole complex pattern of the poem has grown out of twenty lines of Virgil's rhetoric—lines moreover that Chaucer had at first appeared to discard in favour of a revelation of the feelings of an illused woman. Like Virgil's *impia fama* (the 'alltelling Fame' of *Love's Labours Lost*), Rumour has a fearful power of dissemination: *haec passim dea foeda virum diffundit in ora* (*Aen.* iv. 195) . . . *multiplici populos sermones replebat* (189); and what it disseminates is a mixture of false and true: *pariter factaque infecta canebat* (190). Ovid adds the forthright *mendacia* (*Met.* ix. 139) that Chaucer translates as 'lesinges'. And as 'fame' has been credited with the power of revealing what would otherwise be concealed (352), so now we see the poet peering into the mystery of the transmutation of 'tidings' into art as if he were indeed one of those 'spies' of Fame whose existence he had at first rather doubtfully posited (704).

The typical travellers found in this house of Aventure, like the merchant mentioned by the Man of Law, bring their 'tydinges of sondry regnes', their 'wondres' (*C T*, B.

181-2) from abroad—or, like Langland's pilgrims and palmers, compound their 'wise tales' from 'sooth' and 'lesing' (*Piers Plowman*, B, Prol. 46-52). Merely to list their vocations is to suggest the characters into the mouths of whom, as pilgrims to Canterbury, Chaucer is to put just such wonders and tales of 'sondry londes'. Their 'scrippes bretful' (2123) suggest the very figure that comes to Harry Bailly's mind as his scheme for telling tales 'of aventures that whilom han bifalle' begins to burgeon. 'Unbokeled is the male', he cries as the Knight finishes his story (*CT*, A. 3115); when adjuring the parson not to 'breke our *pley*' (cf. *Fame*, 2133) he will bid him 'unbokele and showen what is in thy male' (I. 26); and when the parson characterizes previous tales as 'fables and swich wreccednesse' he is putting them with the 'lesinges' that abound in the house of Aventure, not least on the lips of pardoners whose 'boistes' (2129) prefigure the wallet of the pardoner of Roncesvalles, crammed as it was with false relics on each of which he could hang a tale. If the tale-tellers Chaucer finds in the cage are for the most part dubious or disreputable, so are large numbers of the Canterbury pilgrims themselves. The poet cryptically presents himself as especially anxious to hear a tiding

> That I had herd of som contree
> That shal nat *now* be told for me   (2136-7)

—the tidings, in fact, that the eagle had promised (647-99); and the tales of Canterbury (so many of which are set on foreign strands) may be taken as proof that he ultimately had his desire—whether or no we regard the couplet as alluding to some hearsay knowledge of those prime collections of foreign tales, Boccaccio's *Decameron* or Sercambi's *Novelle*. To tell of this 'now' would be both radically to alter the modest role for which he has cast himself in this poem, and to anticipate the whole comedy that was to be enacted on that sixty-mile route to Canterbury which is as long as the house of Aventure itself (1979). We shall have it all in good time:

> For al mot out, other late or rathe,
> Alle the sheves in the lathe; (2139–40)

The rural phrase, evidently proverbial and answering to the eagle's initial promise of more marvels 'than ever cornes were in graunges' (698), fits happily into the context of the barn-like cage from which all 'tidings' sooner or later escape.[1] But it also confirms the preceding hint that the fullness of the tidings he is concerned with will not be revealed in *this* poem; and so should deter us from curious conjecture about the possibilities of another conclusion to it than the abrupt stop that follows hard upon. Finally, the modest gesture of 'Folk can singe hit bet than I' (2138) conforms to and recalls his earlier disavowal of personal ambition: he has learnt from the adventure in Fame's house not to blow his own trumpet. This passage, in short, crystallizes that specifically Chaucerian detachment which is never cynical or superior, and which is sweetened by an apparent *naïveté* masking moral wisdom.

As if preoccupied with the search for and study of these new tidings, the dreamer does not stir when he hears a great commotion in that corner of the hall where love-stories are being told—where, in fact, the eagle's promise of such tidings is at last, however summarily, fulfilled. It may seem surprising that Chaucer the professed love-poet

---

[1] Chaucer turned regularly to field and farm for images of literary labour: cf. *LGW*, G. 61–64 ('. . . glening here and there . . .') and *CT*, A. 886–7 '. . . (a large feeld to ere'), etc.

does not join the rest of the company as they run *en masse*
to the favoured spot. But he has no need to learn that
'sothsawes' and 'lesinges' are intermeddled in love-stories
as in everything else. To have watched the whirligig of
Rumour was to have seen that everything the Eagle had
avouched about the paradise of love (674) must needs be
true. The bird had spoken of 'mo loves *casuelly* That ben
betid, no man wot why' (679); it is not surprising, then,
to find that stories about them are to be found in this house
of Chance. The very answer 'I not never what' (2148) to
the general question 'What thing is that?' echoes the eagle's
earlier negatives.

The renewed sense in this last scene of crowding and
confusion corresponds to true dream-experience; and it is
all of a piece with the prevalent dream-atmosphere of the
poem that the function of the last of the *dramatis personae*
should remain as mysterious as his relation to the crowds
of tale-mongers. This 'man of gret auctoritee' (2158) is
not, as the poem now stands, identified with the men who
'of love-tidynges tolde' (2143); and since the poet himself
avers that he is no one whom he knew (or even knew of?)
any attempt to unriddle him is supererogatory. It seems
unlikely that he was intended as a *deus ex machina*: the
main action is manifestly over, the eagle has fulfilled his
mission. What little we are told of this commanding figure
suggests an *auctor* with the prestige of the Africanus of the
Parliament, or one of those 'olde wyse' who at the outset
of the *Legend of Good Women* (Chaucer's first collection of
'love-tidings') he associates with

> those olde appreved stories
> Of holinesse, of regnes, of victories,
> Of love, of hate, of other sondry thinges
>   (prol. F. 21-23)

—an asyndetic catalogue which chimes with that we have just had in *Fame* (1961 ff.); love, we note, is but one of many themes, and not the prime one. It would have been consistent with the pattern of Chaucer's other poetry if the work had 'ended in some vertuous sentence'—as the Tales do—or if the dreamer had wakened to some loud external noise or commotion. But in this poem more noise is hardly possible; and to leave the poem (and the poet) suspended in mid-air is to suggest a sudden awakening almost equally well. Moreover three of the Canterbury tales are to break off just as abruptly, one at least of set purpose. The fourteenth century—witness Petrarch's *Trionfi* or the first recension of *Piers Plowman*—was not unaccustomed to such unfinished pieces. In any case the quizzical preface to the poem ought to have half-prepared us for an unusual or unorthodox close. We may feel cheated: but the cheating may be deliberate, and its purpose to suggest that the true conclusion is to be found in the poetry that was to follow—the love-tidings and the tales of 'aventures' that are to make up the bulk of the Canterbury stories, presented as these are essentially as oral narratives.

In one sense, then, God surely did as the poet had besought him and 'turned this dreme to gode' (58). And those reservations about dreams that bulk large in the Proem sort with the implications of this last and liveliest scene; just as the element of parody to be detected there and in other references to dreams and love would hardly be possible if he were accepting unreservedly the literary conventions surrounding those themes.

And in retrospect that opening discourse on the veracity of some dreams, and the unreliability of others, will now appear as proper preface for the dream of Venus in her temple, of Fame in her palace, of 'tidings' in their house of wicker. In each of these abodes, as in men's passion for women, for renown, for story, the true and the false are intermingled. In retrospect, too, the eagle's elaborate unfolding of the 'laws' of sound falls felicitously into place, since these laws pattern the ways in which oral narrative develops; such narrative is the chief stuff of medieval vernacular verse and was certainly hence/ forth to prove the chief strength of Chaucer. In the course of the poem we have left behind the secluded and hermit/ like poet who 'in [Venus's] matere *al* devysest' (637) and come to the ceaseless movement and miscellaneity of the ordinary life of those 'verray neyghebores That dwellen almost at thy dores'. A proper estimate of the importance of 'tidings of love's folk' can now be made: various and manifold as they are, they occupy but one corner (2142) of the great 'lathe' or barn of story. Chaucer is far from abandoning the theme of love. The plight of Dido will lead him to consider the griefs of other 'good women' in like case, and ardent lovers will find their niche in the *Parliament* and in more than one of the Tales. But henceforth love will be seen in the setting of everyday actualities. The formal, intense language of the tercels and the turtledoves will be answered by the earthy colloquial/ isms of wormfowl and waterfowl and by the doctrine that 'there been mo sterres, God wot, than a paire'. Against Troilus's anguish will be set Pandarus's sober realism and easy flow ('From hasel wode, ther Joly Robin pleyde . . .' and so forth). The Knight's high/toned romance, itself seasoned with Theseus's salty phrases, will stand alongside the tale of the popelot Alysoun and the Absolon who 'may blowe the bukkes horn'. A sense of the gain in depth, variety, and richness to be derived from such counterpoises may well have made the poet too impatient to conclude his *Book of Fame*, and too restive to finish the 'seyntes Legendes of Cupide', even though these allowed him more freedom to depict human duplicity than trans-lating the fourth book of the *Aeneid* had done. In the house of tidings and Aventure he had glimpsed the possibilities of a narrative art that could range far beyond the classical and the courtly; and it had even suggested the ideal vehicle for accommodating a medley of stories false and true: the tale of a journeying company (in which he himself was *persona grata*)

> Of sondry folk, by aventure yfalle
> In felawshipe—and pilgrimes were they alle.

Well may the commentator on the *Book of Fame* echo in conclusion the words of Caxton (themselves in part echoing Chaucer's own praise of his Oxford clerk):

I fynde nomore of this werke to foresayd For as fer as I can understonde This noble man Gefferey Chaucer fynysshyd at the sayd conclusion of the metynge of lesyng and sothsawe whereas yet they ben chekked and maye nat departe whyche werke as me semeth is craftyly made and digne to be wreton and knowen. For he towchyth in it ryght grete wysedom & subtyll understondyng And so in alle his werkys excellyth in myn oppynyon alle other wryters in our Englissh For he wrytteth no voyde wordes but alle hys mater is ful of hye and quycke sentence . . .

Additional Notes

p. 17. The passage from Bersuire reads a little differently in the critical edition recently published by J. Engels, in which the last sentence runs: '. . . a deliciarum fluxibus generatur. Ideo cuidam meretrici videtur loqui Scriptura' (*Petrus Berchorius. Reductorium morale, Liber* XV: *Ovidius Moralizatus* cap. I: De Formis. Figurisque Deorum. Textus e codice Brux. Bibl. Reg. 863-9 critice editus. Werkmateriaal (3). Utrecht (1966), p. 23.

All references to Bersuire and the *Libellus de imaginibus deorum* in the present work should be read in the light of the Introduction to this critical edition.

p. 160. The *Collatio pro fine operis* of Bersuire's *Reductorium,* discovered by M. Ch. Samaran (see *Hist. litt. de la France,* t. 39 (1962), p. 302) and edited by Maria van der Bijl (*Vivarium,* iii (1965), no. 2, 149-70), contains a passage embodying the *loci classici* for this doctrine and its converse:

Fama enim et gloria sunt similes cocodrillo, qui sequitur fugientes et effugit insequentes, quia pro certo, sicut dicit Crisostomus omelia iiij: *Si gloriari cupis, gloriam despice, et eris omnibus gloriosor* [cf. P.G. lvii, col. 51]. Et alibi ticit idem: *hec est,* inquit, *glorie gloriosa proprietas, quia fugit se sequentes et sequitur se spernentes:*

O quam nobilis modus famam querendi est fame despeccio seu fuga ! Quod eciam approbat Seneca, quando dicit iii epistula: *Vis omnibus esse notus ? prius fac ut neminem noveris* [Liber de Moribus, no. 37]. *Veni Athenas,* inquit Democritus, *nemo unquam me agnovit. Mirum Athenis cognosci non potuit quem totus mundus cognitums erat.* . . . Sencea etiam loquens Lucillo dicit sic: *Virtus,* inquit, *tua latere non potuit; sequetur te quocumque ieris* multum *pristine lucis: fatuum* [igitur] *iudico famam et laudem querere, quia eciam invitos solet, si digni sunt, occupare* [cf. *Ep. mor.* 19, 4, and 79, 13, 17] (*Vivarium,* loc. cit., 165-6).

Index

PRINTED IN GREAT BRITAIN
AT THE UNIVERSITY PRESS, OXFORD
BY VIVIAN RIDLER
PRINTER TO THE UNIVERSITY